THE
GERMAN NAVY
IN
WORLD WAR II

THE
GERMAN
NAVY
IN
WORLD
WAR II

ROBERT JACKSON

British Library Cataloguing in Publication Data:
A catalogue record for this book is available
from the British Library

ISBN 1-86227-066-X

First published in the UK in 1999 by
Spellmount Limited
The Old Rectory
Staplehurst
Kent TN12 0AZ

1 3 5 7 9 8 6 4 2

Editorial and design: Brown Packaging Books Ltd
Bradley's Close, 74-77 White Lion Street,
London N1 9PF

Editor: Philip Trewhitt
Design: Wilson Design Associates
Picture Research: Ken Botham and Antony Preston

Printed in The Slovak Republic

Picture credits:
Robert Hunt Library: 10, 15, 16, 19, 42, 49, 68, 69, 76, 80, 86,
90, 95, 101, 128, 130-131
Robert Jackson: 73, 144, 151, 156, 157
Antony Preston: 28 (both), 30, 94-95, 102, 103, 105 (both), 107,
113, 115 (bottom), 116, 120, 122, 123, 129, 132, 136, 139, 141,
142, 147, 148, 158
TRH Pictures: front cover, 2-3, 6, 8, 11, 12-13, 14, 18, 21, 22, 22-23,
25, 32, 34, 35, 37, 38, 39, 46, 47, 48, 51, 53, 54, 55, 56-57, 57, 58, 59,
60, 61, 62, 64, 66-67, 70, 72, 79, 82, 83, 87, 89, 93, 96, 106, 110, 112,
115 (top), 117, 118, 124, 138, 145, back cover
Artwork credits:
Aerospace Publishing: 24-25, 40-41, 44-45, 88-89, 98-99, 100, 104,
108-109, 109, 114, 126-127, 134-135, 137, 146, 148-149, 150, 152
Bob Garwood: 20-21, 120-121
Istituto Geografico De Agostini S.p.A.: 26, 26-27, 29, 52-53, 64-65,
74-75, 84-85, 91, 140, 154-155

Previous pages: *Prinz Eugen* opens up with her 8in guns.

CONTENTS

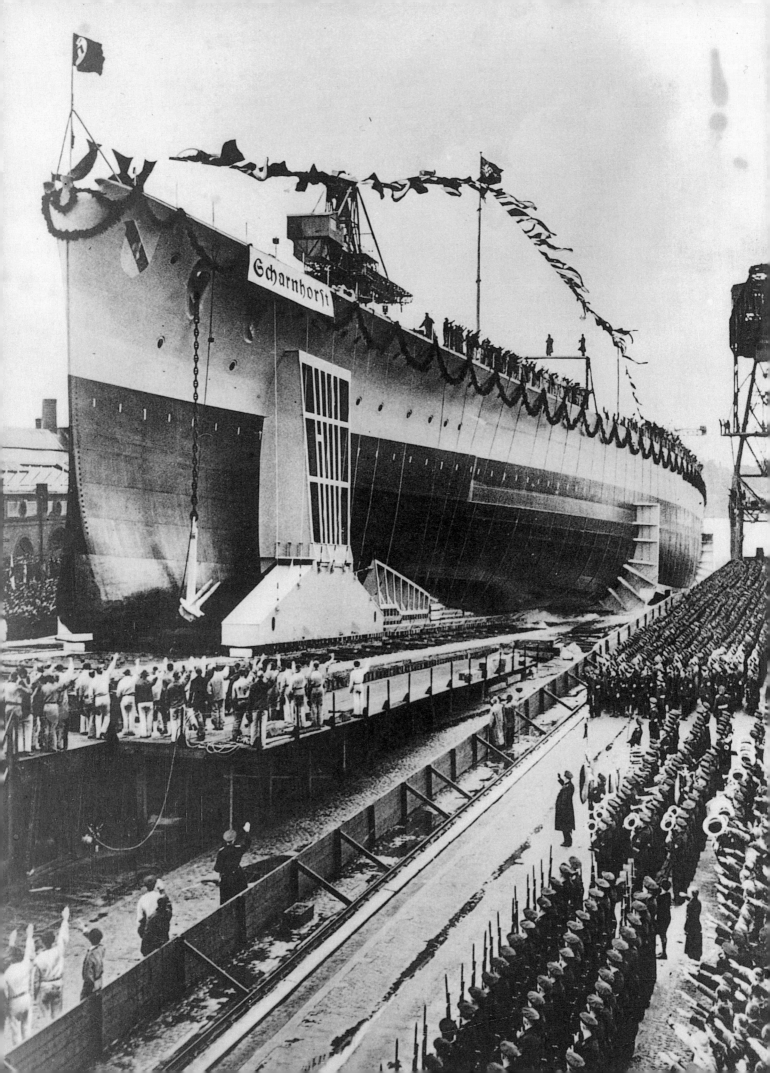

REBIRTH OF A NAVY

The terms of the Versailles Treaty at the end of World War I reduced the former Imperial German Navy to little more than a coastal defence force. The situation was to change dramatically after 1933, when the Nazis came to power and authorised the building of a mighty fleet to challenge Britain's naval supremacy.

When World War I ended in November 1918, the German High Seas Fleet, built primarily to challenge British naval supremacy in the North Sea, remained substantially intact. This was due mainly to the outcome of the Battle of Jutland, fought on 31 May 1916. In this, one of history's major naval engagements, involving 259 warships on both sides, the Royal Navy actually suffered more heavily, losing three battle-cruisers, three armoured cruisers and 6107 men against the Imperial German Navy's loss of one battlecruiser, one old battleship, three armoured cruisers and 3058 men. Yet it was the German High Seas Fleet which broke off the engagement, giving the Royal Navy a strategic victory and

LEFT *The launching of the battlecruiser* Scharnhorst *at Wilhelmshaven on 3 October 1936. Together with her sister ship, the* Gneisenau, *she was to remain a constant thorn in Britain's side until she was sunk off North Cape in December 1943.*

command of the North Sea. After Jutland, the High Seas Fleet played no further part in the war, remaining penned up in its base at Wilhelmshaven.

Under the terms of the Armistice, the German Fleet, which was then in a state of mutiny, was speedily disbanded. The newest and most powerful units of the Fleet – 11 battleships, five battlecruisers, eight cruisers and 50 destroyers – were seized and sailed to Scapa Flow in the Orkneys, where they were interned and subsequently scuttled by their crews in a last gesture of defiance. All the Imperial Navy's submarines were handed over at Harwich.

Of the remaining units of the Fleet, seven cruisers were handed over to the French and Italian Navies; a number of destroyers and submarines were also taken over and decommissioned. Almost all the other vessels were scrapped.

Under the terms of the Peace Treaty, Germany was forbidden to have a submarine fleet or a naval air arm.

ABOVE *The light cruiser* Emden *was the first medium-sized German warship to be built after World War I. Originally coal-fired, she converted to oil-burning engines in 1943 and served throughout World War II. She was constructed at the Wilhelmshaven Dockyard.*

The ships that were permitted to remain in German service were relegated to a coastal defence role and were already obsolete, comprising eight old pre-war battleships, eight light cruisers, 32 destroyers and torpedo boats, some minesweepers and auxiliary craft. The Allies, determined that Germany would never again have warships comparable to those of other navies, stipulated that the size of new German capital ships would not exceed 10,160 tonnes (10,000 tons) displacement and cruisers 6096 tonnes (6000 tons).

It was at this juncture, on 6 February 1922, that the Washington Naval Treaty was signed. The principal aim of the Washington Treaty, which was engineered by the USA and which in effect was the first disarmament treaty in history, was to limit the size of the navies of the five principal maritime powers, which at that time were Britain, the USA, France, Italy and Japan. For Britain, this meant a reduction in capital ship assets to 20 by scrapping existing warships and dropping new projects; however, because her capital ships were older and less heavily armed than those of the USA, she would be permitted to build two new vessels as replacements for existing ones. The other nations would also be permitted to build new capital ships to replace vessels that were 20 years old. This arrangement would allow France and Italy to lay down new warships in 1927, while Britain, the USA and Japan would not need to do so until 1931. No new capital ship was to exceed 35,561 tonnes (35,000 tons), nor mount guns larger than 41cm (16in). No existing capital ship was to be rebuilt, although an increase in deck armour against air attack was allowed, as were the addition of anti-torpedo bulges, provided these modifications did not exceed a total of 3048 tonnes (3000 tons).

The Washington Treaty also limited the tonnage of aircraft carriers. Each signatory nation was allowed to build two vessels of up to 33,530 tonnes (33,000) tons; the remainder were limited to 27,433 tonnes (27,000 tons), and the total aircraft carrier tonnage in the case of Britain and the USA was not to exceed 137,167 tonnes (135,000 tons). Japan was allowed 82,300 tonnes (81,000 tons), while France and Italy were permitted 60,963 tonnes (60,000 tons) each. None of the carriers was allowed an armament in excess of eight 20cm (8in) guns, nor might they be replaced until they were 20 years old. No other warships were to be built in excess of 10,160 tonnes (10,000 tons), nor have guns larger than 20cm (8in).

Meanwhile, outside the orbit of the Washington Treaty, a new German Fleet was being born. The first medium-sized German warship built after World War I was the light cruiser *Emden*, completed in January 1925 at the Wilhelmshaven Dockyard. Originally coal-fired, she converted to oil in 1934. Designed primarily for foreign service, she made nine foreign cruises as a training ship from 1926 and went on to see active service in World War II, carrying out minelaying operations in September 1939 and during the Norwegian campaign of April 1940. She subsequently served with the Fleet Training Squadron in the Baltic and operated in support of the German offensive against the Soviet Union. One of her more unusual operations, in January 1945, was to evacuate the coffin of Field Marshal von Hindenburg from Königsberg, East Prussia, after it had been removed from the Tannenberg Memorial during the Soviet advance into Germany. In April 1945, she was damaged during a bombing raid on Kiel, and was later scuttled. She was broken up in 1949.

In 1924, the construction of 12 new torpedo boats was also started, six of the Wolf class and six of the Möwe (Seagull) class, all at the Wilhelmshaven Dockyard. With a displacement of around 945 tonnes (930 tons), these vessels were powered by two-shaft geared turbines and were capable of 61km/h (33 knots). All were armed with six 53cm (21in) torpedo tubes, three 10.4cm (4.1in) guns and four 20mm (0.79in) anti-aircraft guns. They carried a complement of 129, and all were completed by 1929.

'Pocket battleships'

In that year, a significant step forward was taken with the commencement at the Deutsche Werke, Kiel, of the first of a new class of warship. Designated Panzerschiffe (Armoured Ships) by the Germans, they were to become popularly known as 'Pocket Battleships'. The 11,888-tonne (11,700-ton) *Deutschland* (later renamed *Lützow*) was the first, the others being the Admiral Scheer and the Admiral Graf Spee. Designed from the outset as commerce raiders with a large and economical radius of action – 16,677km (9,000nm) at 35 km/h (19 knots) – they were electrically welded to save weight and equipped with diesel engines. They had enough speed – 48km/h (26 knots) – to enable them to escape from any vessel that could not be overwhelmed by their guns.

Their armament comprised six 28cm (11in) guns, eight 15cm (5.9in) guns, six 10.4cm (4.1in) anti-aircraft guns, eight 37mm (1.44in) anti-aircraft guns, ten (later 28) 20mm (0.79in) anti-aircraft guns and eight 53cm (21in) torpedo tubes. They carried a complement of 1150 crew.

Of enormous significance, too, was the appointment in 1929 of Admiral Erich Raeder to command the Reichsmarine. Raeder had served as a staff officer to Admiral Franz von Hipper in World War I, and had later been assigned the task of writing the official German history of the war at sea. In doing so, for the first time, he had become fully aware of the achievements of the handful of German commerce raiders in distant waters. Not only had they sunk a large tonnage of merchant shipping; they had also tied down many Allied capital ships and cruisers, diverted to search for them.

It was Raeder who authorized the construction of the *Deutschland*'s two sister ships, the *Scheer* and *Graf Spee*. He would almost certainly have ordered more, had it not been for Adolf Hitler's rise to power in 1933 and a subsequent change of naval policy dictated by the new political climate.

The U-boat returns

Meanwhile, in defiance of the Versailles Treaty and under conditions of strict secrecy, Germany had been taking steps to recreate a submarine arm. As early as 1922 a submarine design office was established at Den Haag (The Hague) in the Netherlands under cover of a Dutch firm, and it was under the guise of constructing submarines for foreign navies that the German designers and constructors – which had remained in close touch since the end of World War I – set about producing craft which would actually serve as prototypes for a reborn German submarine service. In 1928–30 they set to work on one submarine for Turkey and five for Finland.

The Turkish craft, the *Gur*, was laid down in Spain in 1932 and furnished with machinery made principally in Holland. In fact, she was the protype for two 876-tonne (862-ton) Type IA U-boats built in 1936, both of which were relegated to training duties at the outbreak of war in 1939. The Finnish submarines were a good deal more interesting; the last of them, the 258-tonne (254-ton) *Vessiko*, was built by the German firm Chrichton-Vulcan AB at Turku on the southwestern tip of Finland and given the designation Submarine 707, although she was actually the prototype for the Type IIA U-boat. To add to her cover story, a rumour was put about that she was destined for Estonia, but this, of course, was not the case.

A German Officer, Commander Barttenburg, and an Engineer Assistant were appointed to the Finnish Naval Staff, and in the spring of 1931 a German crew arrived to take Submarine 707 through her trials. With the exception of four engine-room ratings, the entire crew consisted of young German officers. Every year thereafter, a fresh crew was sent to Finland, and in this way a score of potential U-boat commanders received six months training in the latest attack techniques at the expense of the Finns and without any complaint from the outside world. In the meantime, a 498-tonne (490-ton) ocean-going boat was being tested under the auspices of the Finns; she was the Vetehinen, and she was to serve as the prototype for the main operational U-boat class, the Type VII.

By 1930, all the construction programmes of the maritime powers had been severely affected by economic constraints, the world being in the grip of a savage depression. With the exception of Japan, all the maritime nations were eager to escape the cost of building replacement capital ships, as permitted by the Washington Treaty, and on 22 April 1930 a new treaty, signed in London by the five principal powers, made fresh provisions. Britain, Japan and the USA agreed that they would lay down no new capital ships before 1936, while France and Italy decided to lay down only the two they were already allowed. Furthermore, the first three countries agreed to make further reductions in existing assets; Britain would reduce her force of capital ships to 15 by scrapping HMS *Tiger* and three Iron Duke-class vessels, and relegating the old *Iron Duke* herself to the role of training and depot ship. The USA and Japan also agreed to reduce their capital ship assets to 15 and nine respectively.

Within three years, the Treaties of Washington and London had been torn to shreds by the march of international events. First of all, in 1933, Japan invaded Manchuria, giving notice to the world that she intended to establish domination of the Far East, and then withdrew from the League of Nations. She quickly followed this step with a notice to end her adherence to the Washington and London Treaties, her intention being to establish naval parity with Britain and the USA. France, increasingly alarmed by the growing hostility of fascist

BELOW *The 'pocket battleships'* Admiral Scheer *(foreground) and* Deutschland *at Swinemünde in May 1937. On 29 May, while blockading Spanish ports, the* Deutschland *was bombed by Spanish Republican aircraft. Two days later, the* Scheer *bombarded Almería.*

ABOVE *Nazi leader Adolf Hitler pictured at Kiel in 1933 with Admiral Erich Raeder, Commander-in-Chief of the German Navy. The two later clashed on policy during the war, and Raeder defied Hitler's order to remove Jewish officers from the navy; ironically some served with distinction in World War II, particularly in U-boats.*

Italy, followed suit early in 1935. Also in 1935, and in defiance of the League of Nations, Italy embarked upon a campaign of aggression in Abyssinia; and in 1936 Germany, having repudiated the Treaty of Versailles, seized the Rhineland.

The Nazi Party was now in power in Germany, and one of the first acts of the new Chancellor, Adolf Hitler, was to initiate a massive rearmament programme. As far as the German Navy was concerned, the immediate result was the construction of a new class of Schlachtkreuzer (Battlecruiser). Five ships were projected, but only two were started. The first of these, the 32,514-tonne (32,000-ton) *Scharnhorst*, was laid down at Wilhelmshaven in April 1934; she was followed a year later by the *Gneisenau*.

The design of these powerful warships was based on that of the uncompleted Mackensen class battlecruisers of World War I, which in turn were based on the *Derfflinger* of 1912 – arguably the best battlecruiser of its day. The new ships were fitted with three-shaft geared turbines and their radius of action was 18,530km (10,000nm) at 35 km/h (19 knots). Their armament comprised nine 28cm (11in) guns, 12 15cm (5.9in) guns, 14 10.5cm (4.1in) guns, 37mm (1.44in) anti-aircraft, and 10 (later 38) 20mm (0.78in) anti-aircraft guns, as well as six 53cm (21in) torpedo tubes. Each carried four 'spotter' aircraft and had a complement of 1800. They were capable of a speed of 57km/h (31 knots). *Scharnhorst* was launched in October 1936 and *Gneisenau* in December that year.

In the mid-1930s a new class of Schwerer Kreuzer (heavy cruiser) was also laid down. There were five ships in all, named *Lützow, Seydlitz, Prinz Eugen, Blücher* and *Admiral Hipper*. The first of these, launched in July 1939, was sold in 1940 to the Soviet Navy, in whose service she was successively named *Petropavlovsk* and *Tallinn*. The others were all launched in 1937–39. Capable of 59km/h (32 knots), their armament comprised eight 20cm (8in) guns, 12 10.5cm (4.1in) anti-aircraft guns, 12 37mm (1.44in) anti-aircraft guns, and eight (later 28) 20mm (0.78in) anti-aircraft guns, in addition to 12 53cm (21in) torpedo tubes. Each carried three spotter aircraft. Complement was 1600.

Completing the line-up of Germany's major surface vessels between the two world wars were the light cruisers. The *Emden* of 1925 has already been mentioned; she was followed in 1927 by the *Karlsrühe*, launched in 1927, the *Köln* of 1928 and the *Leipzig* of 1929. Next came the *Nürnberg*, launched in 1934, and the *Königsberg* in 1937. The *Nürnberg* and *Leipzig*, at 6700 tons, were the largest, with a complement of 850. Their armament comprised nine 15cm (5.9in) guns, eight 8.9cm (3.5in) anti-aircraft guns, and eight 37mm (1.44in) anti-aircraft guns, as well as 12 53cm (21in) torpedo tubes, and they had a top speed of 59km/h (32 knots). The others were smaller, displacing 5690 tonnes (5600 tons) and with a complement of 630. They carried an armament of eight 15cm (5.9in), three 8.9cm (3.5in) anti-aircraft and four 37mm (1.44in) anti-aircraft guns, in addition to four 53cm (21in) torpedo tubes. Three other light cruisers, which remained unnamed, were never finished and were broken up on their stocks in 1943, while three more remained projects only.

Anglo-German Agreement

On 20 June 1935, an Anglo-German Agreement was signed. Under its terms, German warship tonnage was restricted to 35 per cent of British equivalents of all classes except submarines, which could be built up to 45 per cent. In effect, this meant that Germany could legitimately build U-boats up to a total of 24,385 tonnes (24,000 tons). At this time, the Royal Navy had 59 submarines in commission, of which 20 were in the 1372 to 1834-tonne (1350 to 1805-ton) range; the rest were between 416 and 680 tonnes (410 and 670 tons), which was about the size the Germans were planning. The Agreement was concluded without consultation with the Dominions, France or the USA, and it is not clear why it was signed at all, unless the British Admiralty mistakenly believed that it would lead to the Germans building 45 per cent of the British total in numbers rather than in tonnage, which would have resulted in only 26 U-boats.

What it actually did was to open the door for a massive increase in Germany's submarine fleet, because 12 254-tonne (250-ton) U-boats had already been laid down before the Agreement was signed and 12 more were to be added during the year.

In July 1935, less than a month after the Anglo-German Agreement was concluded, a certain Captain Karl Dönitz was summoned to Admiral Raeder's office and ordered to assume command of the embryo U-boat

service. Dönitz had served in U-boats during World War I, and although his career had not been very distinguished, he showed exceptional qualities of leadership and organisational ability. Although at first he did not relish the task in hand, he applied himself to it energetically, lobbying for a minimum of 300 submarines to wage unrelenting

war on maritime commerce should it become necessary. In fact, by September 1939, the German Navy had only 56 submarines, of which 46 were in commission, and of these only 22 were ocean-going craft, suitable for service in the Atlantic. They were Type VIIs, with an endurance of 16,400km (8850nm) at 18.5 km/h (10 knots) but capable

ABOVE *German U-boats pictured at Kiel shortly before the outbreak of war in 1939. The boat alongside the accommodation ship is the* U33, *a Type VIIA. She was sunk on the Firth of Clyde on 12 February 1940 by the minesweeper HMS* Gleaner. *The boat on the left,* U34, *was lost in a collision in the Baltic in September 1943.*

ABOVE *The battlecruiser* Scharnhorst *being built at Wilhelmshaven in September 1934. Five vessels in all were planned in this class, but only* Scharnhorst *and* Gneisenau *were completed. Five projected battleships were also cancelled in favour of U-boat building.*

of 31km/h (17 knots). With a conning tower only 5.2m (17ft) above the warterline they were hard to detect even in daylight, and under night conditions they were practically invisible. They could dive in less than half a minute; they could go down to 100m (328ft) without strain and to 200m (656ft) if hard pressed. They could maintain a submerged speed of 14km/h (7.6 knots) for two hours, 7.5km/h (four knots) for 80 hours and 3.5km/h (two knots) for 130 hours. In fact, their depth and endurance performance at high speed was twice as good as in any other submarines. It was with these boats that Dönitz, soon to be promoted to Admiral, would principally fight his underwater battle.

While Dönitz was plotting the expansion of his U-boat fleet, Admiral Raeder and his naval staff were putting the finish touches to a scheme which was designed to give Germany technological superiority on the high seas. It was based on two super-powerful battleships, the *Bismarck*

and *Tirpitz*. Displacing 42,370 tonnes (41,700 tons) in the case of *Bismarck* and 43,589 tonnes (42,900 tons) in the case of *Tirpitz*, they would have a speed of 54km/h (29 knots) and a combat radius of 16,677km (9,000nm) at 35km/h (19 knots). They would carry a formidable armament of eight 38cm (15in) guns, 12 15cm (5.9in) guns, 16 10.5cm (4.1in) anti-aircraft guns, 16 37mm (1.44in) anti-aircraft guns and 16 (later 58) 20mm (0.78in) anti-aircraft guns, together with eight 53cm (21in) torpedo tubes. Their complement would be 2400 officers and men. Both were laid down in 1936, but only the *Bismarck* was launched before the outbreak of World War II.

Six even larger (57,100-tonne/56,200-ton) battleships were planned, known simply by the letters H, J, K, L, M and N. Only H and J were laid down, in 1938, and these were broken up on the stocks in the summer of 1940, at a time when Germany believed she had won the war. It was speculated that they were to be named *Friedrich der Grosse* and *Gross Deutschland*, although there is no concrete evidence for this.

Finally, there were plans to build a small number of aircraft carriers. In the event there was only one, the 23,370-tonne (23,200-ton) *Graf Zeppelin*, laid down in 1936 and launched in December 1938. Her four-shaft geared turbines would have given her a maximum speed of 61km/h (33 knots) and a combat radius of 14,824km (8000nm) at 35km/h (19 knots). It was originally planned that she should carry an air group comprising 12 Junkers Ju 87D dive bombers and 30 Me 109F fighters, later amended to 28 Ju 87Ds and 12 Me 109Gs.

She was never completed. Construction was suspended in May 1940 when she was 85 per cent complete; she was afterwards towed to Gdynia and then to Stettin. In 1942 she went to Kiel, where work on her was restarted; it was again suspended in 1943, after which she was towed to the Oder River and scuttled near Stettin in April 1945. In March 1946 she was raised by the Russians and towed to Swinemunde. In September 1947 she struck a mine and reports differ as to her fate. It is possible that she sank north of Danzig, or she may have been towed to Leningrad, severely damaged, and broken up there.

The hull of a sister vessel was completed up to the armoured deck but she was never launched, being broken up on the stocks in 1940. It was speculated that this ship was to have been named *Peter Strasser*, after the commander of the German Naval Airship Division in World War I.

In 1942 work was also started to convert the heavy cruiser *Seydlitz* as an aircraft carrier, but very little was carried out and the ship was scuttled at Königsberg in April 1945, later being raised by the Russians. Plans were also laid to convert the liners *Europa*, *Gneisenau* and *Potsdam* as an emergency measure, but these came to nothing.

When Germany went to war in 1939, she was at a distinct numerical disadvantage in every respect. Yet during the long years that followed the occupation of Europe, she came close to starving Britain into submission. Her principal weapon in the murderous conflict that became known as the Battle of the Atlantic was the U-boat; but in the early months it was the German Navy's surface vessels that took the greatest toll of Allied shipping.

BELOW *The 43,588-tonne (42,900-ton) battleship Tirpitz, pictured during trials in the Baltic in 1941. Although a constant threat to the Allied convoys, she only once fired her guns in anger against a surface target – the island of Spitzbergen.*

CHAPTER I

THE COMMERCE RAIDERS

During World War I, the Germans learned that one of the best offensive tactics against Britain was to wage war on the merchant fleets that maintained her. The lesson was not lost on Admiral Erich Raeder, whose naval strategy was based on the destruction of Allied shipping in all the world's oceans.

In August 1939, with the invasion of Poland imminent, the German Naval Staff lost no time in deploying units of the Kriegsmarine to their war stations in the Atlantic, ready to begin an immediate offensive against Allied shipping. On 21 August, as part of these movements, the pocket battleship *Admiral Graf Spee* sailed from Wilhelmshaven, under cover of darkness and unobserved, to make rendezvous with her supply ship, the fleet tanker *Altmark*, in the South Atlantic. She was

LEFT *The 'Pocket Battleship'* Admiral Graf Spee *had only a brief career as a commerce raider before she was hunted down by British cruisers and forced to take refuge in the neutral port of Monte Video. She is seen here sailing for the South Atlantic in 1939.*

followed on 24 August by a second pocket battleship, the *Deutschland*, which sailed for her war station south of Greenland, to be joined later by her own replenishment vessel, the fleet tanker *Westerwald*. Within the next 24 hours, signals had been despatched to all German merchant vessels, ordering them to make for home, friendly or neutral ports with all possible speed.

The *Graf Spee*, in particular, was already well-known in naval circles; she was flagship of the German Fleet, and her pre-war activities had included participation in the multi-national Non-Intervention Patrol off Spain during that civil war. In May 1937, she represented the German Navy at Spithead during the naval review to mark the coronation of King George VI. She had an experienced crew under the command of Captain Hans Langsdorff.

By 21 September British naval intelligence was aware that the two powerful 'pocket battleships' were at sea, and by 5 October, the Admiralty, in conjunction with the French Navy, had formed eight Atlantic 'hunting groups' of aircraft carriers and cruisers for the defence of the trade routes against surface raiders. Three were under the orders of the Commander-in-Chief, South Atlantic, whose headquarters were at Freetown, Sierra Leone; one of them, Group G, comprising the heavy cruisers *Exeter* and *Cumberland* and reinforced later by the light cruisers *Ajax* and *Achilles*, the latter belonging to the Royal New Zealand Navy, was responsible for the waters off the east coast of South America.

The *Graf Spee* sank her first merchantman, the British steamer *Clement*, off Pernambuco on 30 September, and between 5 and 12 October she sank four more before breaking off to replenish from her supply ship, the *Altmark*. She turned up again on 15 November, when she sank a small tanker in the Mozambique Channel. There was no further news of her until 2 December, when she

ABOVE *Crewmen from the torpedoed merchant vessel* Kensington Court *rowing towards a Sunderland flying boat of RAF Coastal Command, one of two which arrived to rescue them. All 34 crew members were saved from the stricken ship, which was sunk on 21 September 1939.*

sank the freighters *Doric Star* and *Tairoa* between St Helena and South Africa.

On receiving intelligence of these sinkings, the C-in-C South Atlantic, Vice-Admiral d'Oyly Lyon, ordered Force H, with the cruisers *Shropshire* and *Sussex*, to proceed to the area between Cape Town and St Helena, while Force K, comprising the battlecruiser *Renown*, the aircraft carrier *Ark Royal* and the cruiser *Neptune*, was despatched to search along a line from Freetown to the Central South Atlantic. Force G (as Group G was now designated) meanwhile assembled off the River Plate with the cruisers *Achilles, Ajax and Exeter, Cumberland* having been detached to cover the Falkland Islands. There was plenty of mercantile traffic around the estuary of the River Plate, and Force G's senior officer, Commodore H. Harwood, reasoned that Langsdorff would be attracted there sooner or later. He was right.

After sinking two more ships in mid-ocean, Captain Langsdorff elected to steer directly for the Plate estuary, where the *Graf Spee* was sighted by Force G at 0608 hours on 13 December. The three British cruisers were soon in action against her, opening fire from different directions. Langsdorff at first divided his armament, but then concentrated his fire on the *Exeter*, his 28cm (11in) shells inflicting heavy damage on the cruiser. Despite this, Captain F.S. Bell continued to engage the enemy throughout the night, at the end of which the *Exeter* had only one turret left in action and she was ablaze. Langdorff could easily have finished her off; instead, he made smoke and turned west, allowing *Exeter* to pull away to the southeast to make repairs, with 61 of her crew dead and 23 wounded.

The pocket battleship now steered for the coast of Uruguay, under fire all the while from the light cruisers *Ajax* and *Achilles*. At 0725 hours a 30cm (12in) shell hit *Ajax* and put both her after-turrets out of action, but again Langsdorff failed to take the opportunity to finish off one of his adversaries, whose remaining guns were now barely superior to his own secondary armament. The two cruisers continued to shadow the *Graf Spee*, which fired salvoes at them from time to time, until the battleship entered the estuary; Commodore Harwood then called off the pursuit and set up a patrol line, aware that he was in a very parlous position if Langsdorff chose to fight his way out to the open sea.

Langsdorff, his ship damaged - she had taken some 70 hits and 36 of her crew were dead, with another 60 wounded - had decided to make for a neutral port where he could effect temporary repairs before attempting a breakout into the North Atlantic and a run back to Germany. He was also short of ammunition. The *Graf Spee* reached Montevideo in the evening of 14 December, and there now began a prolonged diplomatic effort to remain in port beyond the legal limit of 72 hours, since the necessary repairs would take an estimated two weeks to complete. British propaganda, mean-

while, went all out to create the impression that a large British fleet was lying in wait to ambush the *Graf Spee* as soon as she re-emerged from the La Plata estuary. The aircraft carrier *Ark Royal* and the battlecruiser *Renown* were reported to be at Rio de Janeiro; in fact, they were 4630km (2500nm) away, and the cruiser force had been reinforced by only one more ship, another cruiser, HMS *Cumberland*.

Langsdorff fell for it. On 16 December he sent the following signal to Berlin:

1. Strategic position off Montevideo: Besides the cruisers and destroyers, *Ark Royal* and *Renown*. Close blockade at night. Escape into open sea and breakthrough to home waters hopeless.

2. Propose putting out as far as neutral boundary. If it is possible to fight our way through to Buenos Aires, using remaining ammunition, this will be attempted.

3. If a breakthrough would result in certain destruction of *Graf Spee* without opportunity of damaging enemy, request decision on whether the ship should be scuttled in spite of insufficient depth in the estuary of the La Plata, or whether internment is to be preferred.

RIGHT *An exhausted, oil-smothered survivor of a torpedoed British merchant ship pictured on the Royal Navy destroyer that rescued him. Over 5000 Allied merchant ships were sunk in World War II and the British Merchant Navy lost 30,248 men in action.*

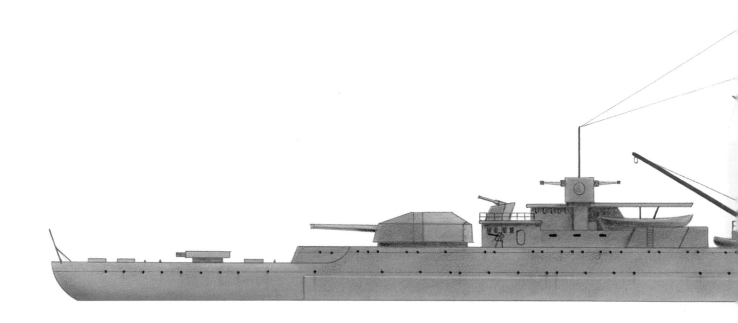

SPECIFICATIONS: *ADMIRAL SCHEER*

GENERAL

Ship type: 'Pocket Battleship'

Entered service: 1934

Complement: 926

Fate: Capsized in dock at Kiel after being damaged by British bombs (32 dead)

MACHINERY

Engine: Diesel

Power: Twin screw

ARMOUR

Belt: 50–80mm (2–3in)

Deck: 18–40mm (0.7–1.5in)

Turrets: 140mm (5.5in)

ARMAMENT

Main: Six 280mm (11in) guns

Secondary: Eight 150mm (96in) guns; three 88mm (3.5in) AA guns; eight 533mm (21in) torpedo tubes

DIMENSIONS

Length: 186m (610ft 3in)

Width: 20.7m (67ft 9in)

Height: 7.2m (23ft 9in)

Displacement: 12,294 tonnes (12,100 tons)

PERFORMANCE

Speed: 48km/h (26 knots)

The reply that came back from Berlin was unequivocal. There was to be no question of internment. The authority was given to scuttle the ship, should the German envoy in Montevideo fail to gain an extension of the time limit in neutral waters. By nightfall on 17 December, it was plain that no such extension was to be permitted by the Uruguayan authorities. On the following morning, watched by a vast crowd of sightseers, *Graf Spee* put to sea. The British warships cleared for action, but before they could engage the enemy, their spotter aircraft reported that the *Graf Spee* had been scuttled and blown up by her own crew. Within a short time, it was learned that Captain Langsdorff had committed suicide.

The *Graf Spee*'s crew were later transferred to Argentina, where they were interned. They remained there until February 1946, when 900 (some having chosen to stay in South America) were repatriated to Germany on the liner *Highland Monarch* – escorted, in a nice touch of irony, by *HMS Ajax*.

In the early weeks of 1940, with the Baltic remaining icebound for an unusually long period, the Germans made increasing use of the alternative route via the north Norwegian port of Narvik to ship Swedish iron ore, a commodity vital to Germany's war industries. The British Admiralty laid plans to extend its blockade to enemy merchant shipping making the long sea passage down Norway's coastline, but this was difficult to implement; for most of the route, the cargo vessels were able to remain inside Norwegian territorial waters by using the narrow passages between the mainland and the offshore

ABOVE *The* Admiral Scheer *was the* Graf Spee*'s sister ship. She saw considerable action against Allied convoys in the Atlantic and Arctic, and provided fire support for German ground forces in the Baltic. In all, she sank 17 ships, including the* Jervis Bay.

BELOW *The* Admiral Graf Spee *at the Spithead Naval Review, May 1937, to mark the coronation of King George VI. Just visible in the background is the Russian battleship* Petropavlovsk, *which was severely damaged by German dive-bombers in 1941.*

home. Passing through the Denmark Strait and entering Norwegian territorial waters, the *Altmark* had been intercepted by a Norwegian torpedo boat, but Dau had refused to allow his ship to be searched.

On 15 February, Admiral Sir Charles Forbes, C-in-C Home Fleet, learned that the *Altmark* was off Bergen, and instructed Captain Q.D. Graham of the cruiser *Arethusa*, returning with five destroyers from a sortie into the Skagerrak, to intercept her. She was sighted the next day, steaming down the Leads, but attempts by the British destroyers to close with her were frustrated by Norwegian torpedo boats steaming close alongside. Darkness found the enemy tanker in Josingfjord, where she was followed by Captain Philip Vian in the destroyer *Cossack*. Informing the senior Norwegian officer that there were British prisoners on the *Altmark*, Vian demanded the right to search for them; the Norwegian commander replied that he was under orders to resist,

ABOVE *Close-up of the* Graf Spee*'s heavily armoured control tower, taken by a US Navy photographer while the ship lay in Montevideo harbour. The Americans and the British were particularly interested in the German 'Seetakt' naval gunlaying radar, the antenna of which is visible at the top.*

islands known as the Inner Leads. The use of Norwegian ports by enemy blockade runners was also a sore point, and matters in this respect came to a head when, on 14 February 1940, the tanker *Altmark* – the *Graf Spee*'s supply ship, carrying some 300 merchant seamen from vessels sunk by the pocket battleship – sought refuge in Trondheim under Norwegian protection.

The *Altmark*'s Captain Dau had ignored Captain Langsdorff's order to land his captives at a neutral port, and instead had remained in the South Atlantic until a signal from Berlin advised him that it was safe to run for

and trained his torpedo tubes on the destroyer. Vian withdrew and sought instructions from the Admiralty. Three hours later, the orders came through from Winston Churchill, then First Lord of the Admiralty.

'Unless Norwegian torpedo-boat undertakes to convoy Altmark to Bergen with a joint Anglo-Norwegian guard on board, and a joint escort, you should board Altmark, liberate the prisoners, and take possession of the ship pending further instructions. If Norwegian torpedo-boat interferes, you should warn her to stand off. If she fires upon you, you should not reply unless attack is serious, in which case you should defend yourself, using no more force than is necessary, and ceasing fire when she desists.'

For the equally resolute Vian, it was enough. Persuading the Norwegian vessels to withdraw, he took the *Cossack* into Josingfjord and went alongside the *Altmark*, evading an attempt by Dau to ram him, and sent over a boarding party. Six Germans were killed and six wounded before they escaped ashore, leaving the British free to break open the *Altmark*'s hatches. Someone asked if there were any British below, and a tremendous yell assured him that the prisoners were all British. The words that followed have become a firm part of British naval tradition: 'Come on up, then – the Navy's here!'

While the *Graf Spee* was on the rampage in the South Atlantic, her sister ship, the *Deutschland* (Captain

BELOW *The end of the* Graf Spee, *scuttled off Montevideo on 17 December 1939. Captain Hans Langsdorff shot himself; his crew were taken to Argentina and were interned there for the duration of the war. During her foray into the Atlantic, the* Graf Spee *sank or captured nine merchant ships.*

Wenneker), was patrolling the Bermuda-Azores route, and on 5 October 1939 she sank the steamer *Stonegate*. A week later she was operating farther north, on the Halifax (Nova Scotia)-UK route, and between 9 and 16 October she sank the Norwegian freighter *Lorentz W. Hansen* and captured the American freighter *City of Flint*, carrying supplies for Britain, a cargo which the Germans described as 'contraband'. On 17 October the German Naval Staff issued an order permitting the use of all weapons against all enemy merchant ships with the exception of passenger vessels, giving the commerce raiders a much wider scope.

On 5 November, however, the *Deutschland* received a sudden recall order from the German Admiralty. Successfully evading British patrols, she slipped through the Denmark Strait, passed to the east of the Shetland Islands and arrived at Gdynia on 17 November, where she went into dry dock for an overhaul. Shortly before docking her captain received word that his ship had been renamed *Lützow*, the cruiser of that name having been

sold to the Soviet Union, and in February 1940 she was reclassified as a heavy cruiser.

The third pocket battleship, the *Admiral Scheer*, was similarly reclassified. She had taken no part in the early commerce-raiding operations; having survived an attack by RAF Blenheim bombers on 4 September 1939 (three bombs hit her while she lay at anchor in Wilhelmshaven, but all failed to explode) she underwent a refit and did not begin operations until October 1940; these will be covered in a later chapter.

A new threat

Although the destruction of the *Graf Spee* and the return to port of the *Deutschland* had significantly reduced the threat to British merchant shipping, another menace loomed large in March 1940 with the deployment of the auxiliary cruiser *Atlantis*. By the end of 1940, six more were deployed: the *Orion, Widder Thor, Pinguin, Komet* and *Kormoran*. All were merchant ships converted to auxiliary cruisers with heavy concealed armament, so

SPECIFICATIONS: *DEUTSCHLAND*

GENERAL

Ship type: Heavy Cruiser

Entered service: 1933

Complement: 1150

Fate: Scuttled 4 May 1945

MACHINERY

Engine: Diesel

Power: Three shafts

ARMOUR

Belt: 57-76mm (2.25-3in)

Deck: 38mm (1.5in)

Turrets: 82.5-138mm (3.25-5.5in)

ARMAMENT

Main: Six 280mm (11in) guns

Secondary: Eight 150mm (96in) guns; three 88mm (3.5in) AA guns; eight 533mm (21in) torpedo tubes

DIMENSIONS

Length: 186m (610ft 3in)

Width: 20.7m (67ft 9in)

Height: 7.2m (23ft 9in)

Displacement: 12,294 tonnes (12,100 tons)

SPEED: 48km/h (26 knots)

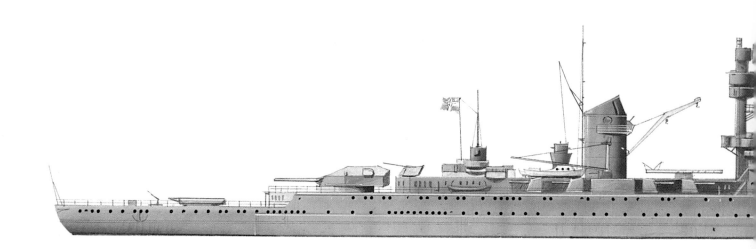

that they retained their merchant ship appearance. The Germans had used similar vessels with great success during World War I, and the success was to be repeated by this new generation. Replenishing from supply ships at secret ocean rendezvous points, they preyed only on solitary unescorted vessels sailing the world's oceans. The British Admiralty's answer to these commerce raiders

ABOVE AND LEFT *The* Deutschland *made a sortie into the Atlantic in October 1939, sinking two merchant ships and capturing a third. She was later renamed* Lützow *and reclassified as a heavy cruiser (Hitler did not want to risk a ship bearing Germany's name to be sunk). She was twice torpedoed, once by a British submarine and once by an aircraft. She was sunk by RAF bombers in 1945.*

was to launch a major search for them using Armed Merchant Cruisers, 50 of which had been converted from fast liners. They were unarmoured and underarmed, and no match for their adversaries.

Commerce raiders

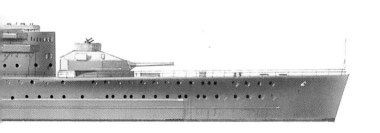

Each German raider had at least five identities: her original merchant name; a naval number prefaced HSK (Handels-Stor-Kreuzer, or Commerce Raiding Cruiser), given to her when she underwent conversion; a ship number prefaced 'Schiff' for communication purposes; her name as a raider, mostly chosen by her captain; and a distinguishing letter allocated by the British Admiralty, once the raider had been discovered. In this way the *Goldenfels*, built originally for the Hansa Line, became

HSK2 Schiff 16 *Atlantis*, known as Raider C to the British because she was the third to be identified, even though she had been the first to sail. *Atlantis*, displacing 7988 tonnes (7862 tons) was armed with six 15cm (5.9in) guns and one 7.62cm (3in) gun, two 37mm (1.44in) and two 20mm (0.79in) anti-aircraft guns, and four 53cm (21in) torpedo tubes. She also carried two Heinkel He 114 floatplanes. She could make 29km/h (16 knots) and her complement was 350.

She set out on 31 March 1940 and headed for the South Atlantic, one of her first tasks being to lay a mine-field off the South African coast. Between 10 June and 20 September she captured or sank seven Allied merchant ships totalling 49,786 tonnes (49,338 tons) in the South Atlantic and Indian Oceans, and also sank the French pas-

BELOW *Formerly* Goldenfels *of the Hansa Line,* Atlantis*'s speed made her ideal for a commerce raiding role. Her onboard arsenal was formidable: she carried two scout planes and 93 mines, as well as acting as a supply vessel for U-boats. She was sunk by the British cruiser* Devonshire *in 1941.*

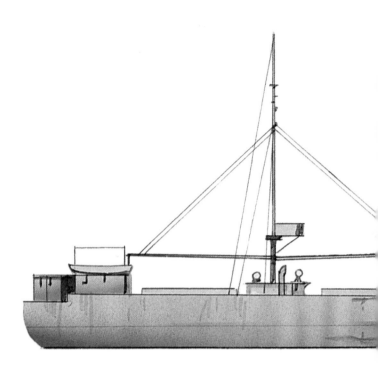

SPECIFICATIONS: *ATLANTIS*

GENERAL
Ship type: Commerce Raider
Entered service: December 1939
Complement: 350
Fate: Sunk by *Devonshire* 23/11/41

MACHINERY
Engine: Diesel
Power: Twin screw

ARMOUR
None

ARMAMENT
Main: Six 150mm (5.9in) guns
Secondary: Two 37mm (1.5in) and two 20mm (0.78in) AA guns; four 53cm (21in) torpedo tubes; 93 mines

DIMENSIONS
Length: 148m (486ft)
Width: 18.5m (61ft)
Height: 9.5m (32ft)
Displacement: 7988 tonnes (7862tons)

PERFORMANCE
Speed: 33km/h (18 knots)

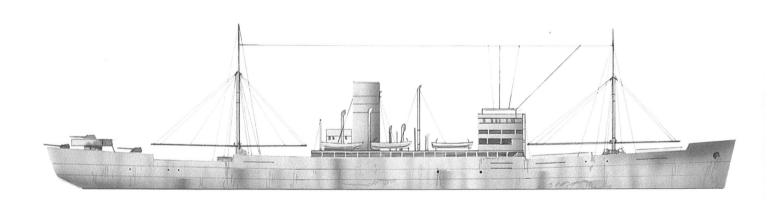

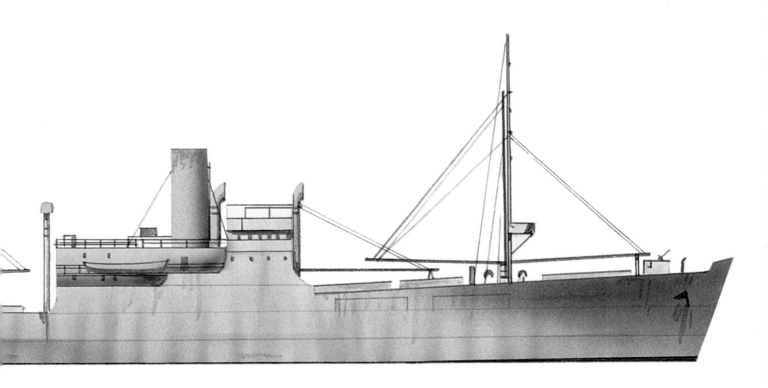

SPECIFICATIONS: *KOMET*

GENERAL

Ship type: Commerce Raider

Entered service: 1940

Complement: 270

Fate: Torpedoed by MTB236 14/10/42

MACHINERY

Engine: Diesel

Power: Single screw

ARMOUR

None

ARMAMENT

Main: Six 150mm (5.9in) guns

Secondary: One 60mm (2.4in) gun; two 37mm (1.5in); four 20mm (0.78in) AA guns; six 53cm (21in) torpedo tubes; 270 mines

DIMENSIONS

Length: 115m (377ft)

Width: 15.3m (50ft 2in)

Height: 6.5m (21ft 4in)

Displacement: 3400 tonnes (3287 tons)

PERFORMANCE

Speed: 29km/h (16 knots)

ABOVE *The German commerce raider* Komet, *formerly the* Ems *of the Norrdeutscher Lloyd Line. She made one raiding voyage, lasting an epic 510 days, and sank 11 ships, seven of which were shared with the Orion. She was sunk as she set out on her second raiding sortie.*

senger liner *Commissaire Ramel*, serving under the British flag. Between 24 January and 2 February 1941, *Atlantis* sank one freighter and captured two others – totalling 17,615 tonnes (17,329 tons) – off the Seychelles, and in March she was engaged in replenishing Italian submarines en route from the Red Sea to the French Atlantic ports via the Cape of Good Hope.

April 1941 found her back in the South Atlantic, where she sank the Egyptian passenger ship *Zamzam* and took the whole crew captive, together with 138 American passengers. A month later, she had a lucky escape when she sailed within 7km (4nm) of the British battleship *Nelson* and the aircraft carrier *Ark Royal* at night without being detected.

Her luck finally ran out on 22 November 1941, by which time she had sunk 22 Allied ships totalling 148,035 tonnes (145,697 tons) in a voyage lasting 622 days. She was replenishing the German submarine *U126* north of Ascension Island when she was surprised by the British heavy cruiser *Devonshire* and forced to scuttle herself

after being heavily shelled. Lieutenant-Commander Bauer of the *U126*, having submerged nearby, waited until the cruiser had departed and then surfaced to take the lifeboats bearing Atlantis's survivors in tow, handing them over to the submarine supply ship *Python* which was summoned to the scene. The latter was herself sunk by the cruiser *Dorsetshire* on 1 December, the survivors reaching home after a rescue operation by German and Italian submarines.

The next commerce raider to sail after *Atlantis*, on 6 April 1940, was HSK1 Schiff 36 *Orion* (Commander

ABOVE *The German commerce raider* Komet *was the smallest of Germany's armed merchant cruisers. She was armed with six 150mm (5.9in) guns and carried a torpedo boat and two scout planes (one of which can be seen on the foredeck).*

BELOW *The German commerce raider* Kormoran *sank the Australian cruiser HMAS* Sydney *during a gun duel on 19 November 1941, but was herself badly damaged and had to be abandoned. Her operational area was the Indian Ocean where she sank 11 ships.*

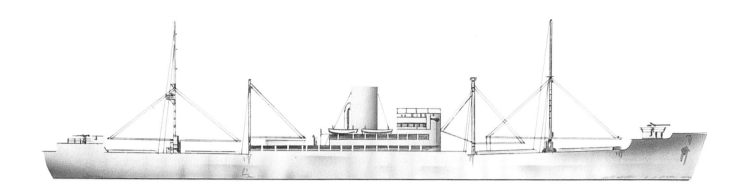

SPECIFICATIONS: *KORMORAN*

GENERAL

Ship type: Commerce raider

Entered service: 1940

Complement: 400

Fate: Sunk by HMAS *Sydney* 19/11/41

MACHINERY

Engine: Diesel

Power: Single shaft

ARMOUR

None

ARMAMENT

Main: Six 150mm (5.9in) guns

Secondary: Four 37mm (1.5in) and four 20mm (0.78in) AA guns; four 53cm (21in) torpedo tubes; 320 mines; one torpedo boat

DIMENSIONS

Length: 164m (538ft)

Width: 20m (66ft 3in)

Height: 8.5m (27ft 10in)

Displacement: 8876 tonnes (8736 tons)

PERFORMANCE

Speed: 33km/h (18 knots)

ABOVE *The* Kormoran's *tally of 11 ships was achieved in a voyage lasting 352 days. This emphasises one of the commerce raiders' most important advantages – their ability to remain at sea for long periods and therefore operate over wide areas. This, combined with considerable firepower, made for dangerous vessels.*

Weyher), which headed for the Pacific. Her first task was to lay minefields on the shipping lanes in New Zealand waters, which she accomplished in June before going on to sink seven ships. In November she made rendezvous with HSK7 Schiff 45 *Komet* (Captain Eyssen), which had sailed from Bergen on 9 July 1940 and reached her operational area in the Pacific by way of the Siberian sea route, her passage assisted by Soviet icebreakers. Together, the two raiders sank a further seven vessels. The German ships then parted company and *Orion* added two more merchantmen to her tally before heading for home. She reached Bordeaux in August 1941 after a voyage that had lasted a total of 510 days. In 1942 she was turned into a floating workshop, and in 1944, renamed *Hektor*, she became a gunnery training ship. She did not survive the war, being bombed and sunk at Swinemünde on 4 May 1945.

Komet arrived back at Hamburg in November 1941, also after a 510-day voyage, having added three more ships to her score. On 7 October 1942, she sailed from Flushing on a second voyage, but a week later she was torpedoed and sunk off the Cap de la Hague, France, by the British motor torpedo boat MTB236 with the loss of all her crew, including her commander, Captain Brocksien.

The third raider to sail, Commander von Ruckteschell's HSK3 Schiff 21 *Widder* (Ram) set out on 6 May 1940, bound for the central Atlantic, where in a voyage of 179 days she sank or captured 10 ships totalling 59,586 tonnes (58,645 tons). From 1941 she was a floating workshop in Norwegian waters; in May 1945 she was seized by Britain, where she was renamed *Ulysses* until being returned to Germany in 1953 under the name *Fechenheim*.

Two raiders sailed in June 1940, the first being HSK4 Schiff 10 *Thor* under Captain Kähler. Her operational area was also the Atlantic, where in a voyage of 329 days she sank or captured 12 ships totalling 98,096 tonnes (96,547 tons), including the British armed merchant cruiser *Voltaire*. In November 1941 she set out on a second cruise, under the command of Captain Gumprich and bound for the Pacific Ocean. On this voyage she sank or captured ten ships totalling 56,936 tonnes (56,037 tons). On 30 November 1942, while at in port at Yokohama, Japan, she was destroyed when the adjacent tanker *Uckermark* (formerly the *Altmark*) caught fire and blew up.

The other raider to sail in June, HSK5 Schiff 33 *Pinguin* (Captain Krüder) was the most successful of all in terms of ships sunk, narrowly beating *Atlantis* in terms of tonnage. Her first operational area was the Indian Ocean, where by mining and direct action she sank nine ships before proceeding to the Antarctic, where her mission was to attack the Norwegian whaling fleet. She was brilliantly successful, capturing two factory ships and 11 whalers, all but three of which reached French Atlantic ports in March 1941 with 22,556 tonnes (22,200 tons) of whale oil on board.

In all, during her 321-day voyage, *Pinguin* was responsible for the destruction of 32 ships totalling 157,100 tonnes (154,619 tons). Her own turn came on 8 May 1941, when she was intercepted off the Seychelles by the heavy cruiser HMS *Cornwall* and sunk with the loss of 18 officers and 323 men. Unfortunately, about 200 prisoners also went down with her. The *Cornwall*

rescued three officers, 57 seamen and 22 prisoners of war.

The last raider to sail in 1940, on 3 December, was HSK8 Schiff 41 *Kormoran* (Commander Detmers), heading for the Atlantic and the Indian Ocean. In a voyage lasting 352 days she sank or captured 11 ships of 69,359 tonnes (68,264 tons) before she was intercepted by the Royal Australian Navy's light cruiser *Sydney* on 19 November, 1941, about 315km (170nm) west of Shark Bay, Western Australia. The German captain managed to prolong the signal exchanges between the two ships until the Sydney had approached close to the *Kormoran*, at which point Detmers abandoned all pretence of disguise and opened fire with all guns. The Australian cruiser, badly hit by the first salvoes and also by a torpedo strike in the bow, limped away over the southern horizon, burning fiercely, and was never seen again. But the

BELOW The Hansa *was taken over by Germany in 1940 and renamed* Meersburg *for service with the Hamburg Amerika Line. She was converted to the commerce raiding role in 1942, but never broke out and was used as a gunnery training ship. She was damaged by a mine in the Baltic on 4 May 1945.*

Kormoran was also doomed; with her pumps out of action, her crew were unable to extinguish an oil fire which soon blazed out of control, forcing the Germans to abandon ship. Soon afterwards, the raider's cargo of mines exploded. Most of the crew reached the Australian coast.

There were no new sailings in 1941. The next was not until 13 March 1942, when HSK9 Schiff 28 *Michel*, with the experienced Commander von Ruckteschell in command, left Flushing en route for the Pacific. In 505 days of sea time she sank or captured 18 ships totalling 129,147 tonnes (127,107 tons). She spent two months in the spring of 1943 undergoing a refit at Kobe, Japan, Captain Gumprich assuming command in the meantime, and August-September of that year found her operating in mid-Pacific. On 7 October she began the return voyage to Japan, and 10 days later she was sunk by three torpedoes from the US submarine *Tarpon*, 167km (90nm) east of Yokohama. 116 of her crew survived.

On 12 May 1942, HSK6 Schiff 23 *Stier* (Commander Gerlach) left Rotterdam on the first stage of a daring dash through the English Channel, escorted by torpedo boats and minesweepers. She succeeded in breaking out into the Atlantic, where during the next four months she sank four ships totalling 29,878 tonnes (29,406 tons). The last, which she encountered unexpectedly in poor visibility on 27 September 1942, was the 7296-tonne (7181-ton) US freighter *Stephen Hopkins* (Captain Paul Buck). Although the freighter was sunk, the return fire from her solitary 10cm (4in) gun was so fierce and accurate during the engagement that the *Stier* was heavily damaged and had to be abandoned, her crew being picked up by the blockade-runner *Tannenfels*.

The last sortie

On 10 February 1943 Schiff 14 *Coronel* (Captain Thienemann) also attempted to break out into the Atlantic through the Channel, but on 13 February she was attacked by Westland Whirlwind fighter-bombers off Gravelines and was forced to put into Boulogne after receiving damage. On 14 February, after surviving further air attacks, she returned to Kiel via Dunkirk and later served as a fighter direction ship in the Baltic. After the war she became a Norwegian auxiliary vessel under the name of Svalbard.

So ended, in failure, the last attempt to send a German auxiliary cruiser into the Atlantic. One other vessel, Schiff 5 *Hansa*, which was under construction in Copenhagen for the UK Glen shipping line when the Germans seized

her in 1940, was also converted, but never sailed on a raiding sortie. After the war she was used by the British Merchant Service, first as the *Empire Humber* and later *Glengarry* – her original intended name.

In the early months of the war, quite apart from the disruption caused by the deployment – or suspected deployment – of Germany's commerce raiders, their impact on the Allied merchant fleets could not be underestimated. In 1940 alone, they sank 54 merchantmen of 375,938 tonnes (370,000 tons), and although this was less than the tonnage lost from air attacks, mines or submarines in the same period, the psychological effect of the raiders' frequent and widespread appearances was enormous.

Attack from the air

Although the auxiliary cruisers remained a constant thorn in the flesh of the British Admiralty, German aircraft presented the main threat to Atlantic and North Sea traffic in the first half of 1941, causing the heaviest losses. In April alone, they sank 116 ships totalling 323,000 tons, their highest figure of the whole war. The unit principally responsible for the losses was KG40. This unit, whose four-engined Focke-Wulf FW 200 Kondor aircraft operated from Bordeaux and Stavanger and ranged far to the west of Ireland, seeking targets of opportunity and providing reconnaissance facilities for the U-boat packs. KG40 had already enjoyed substantial success, claiming 363,000 tons of Allied shipping between August 1940 and February 1941. From 1 January 1941, KG40 came under the direct control of the Fliegerführer Atlantik, a naval command.

The FW 200 threat began to diminish somewhat with the establishment of No 252 Squadron RAF at Aldergrove, in Northern Ireland, in the spring of 1941; equipped with long-range, heavily armed Bristol Beaufighters, the squadron and its successors formed a barrier of sorts between the German bombers and the convoys they were threatening, but their effectiveness was hampered in the early days by the reluctance of the RAF to allow the convoy escorts to communicate directly with the aircraft – an amazing blunder. This meant many interception chances were missed. It was not until the middle of 1941 that the short-sightedness and narrow-minded approach that was proving a bar to effective communication was removed and a form of fighter direction procedure was instituted. The results were quickly evident with a resulting reduction in merchant shipping losses from enemy aircraft.

CHAPTER 2

GERMANY'S BATTLESHIPS

For Germany, the introduction of the new battleships came too late. The German Naval Command had not anticipated going to war until at least 1944: had that been the case, the battleships that were either being built or were in the planning stage in the late 1930s would have formed the nucleus of powerful battle groups.

It must have seemed somewhat ironic to veterans of the Imperial German Navy, left by the Allies with only a handful of obsolete vessels at the end of the 1914-18 war, that the first naval shots of a new conflict should be fired by one of them.

At dawn on 1 September 1939, the old pre-Dreadnought battleship *Schleswig-Holstein*, a vessel that had fought at Jutland and later served successively as a depot vessel and cadet training ship, opened fire with her four 280mm (11in) guns on the Polish fortress of Westerplatte, whose garrison was holding out stubbornly

LEFT *The battleship* Bismarck *firing a salvo from her main armament. The photo was taken in daylight; the dark effect is caused by the vivid flash of the warship's guns. At this time (May 1941), the* Bismarck *was the most powerful warship afloat.*

against the invading Germans. Together with smaller vessels, she continued to shell the fortress day after day for a week, until the garrison at last surrendered on 7 September under the combined effects of the naval shell-fire, air attack and an assault from the ground. The old battleship continued to support the attacking German troops, bombarding Polish positions and batteries near Hochredlau on the Hela peninsula, when she withdrew for replenishment until 13 September; when she returned, on 25 September, it was in the company of her sister ship, the *Schlesien*, together with whom she continued the bombardment for a further two days.

The old battleships' war was not yet over. In April 1940, the *Schleswig-Holstein* led a battle group covering transport vessels that were landing troops in Norway, while the *Schlesien* operated in Danish waters, ready to lend supporting fire as necessary. Afterwards, the

Schleswig-Holstein returned to Gdynia on the Baltic, where she resumed her training role. She was still there on the night of 18-19 December 1944, when Avro Lancasters of RAF Bomber Command dropped 824 tons of bombs on the port, sending the *Schleswig-Holstein* and several other vessels to the bottom.

The *Schlesien* continued to be active in the Baltic, where in March and April 1945 her guns were turned on the Soviet armies advancing on Danzig. She survived almost to the end. On 2 May, in action against Soviet forces in the Swinemünde area, she struck a British-laid air mine and had to be beached at Swinemünde, where her wreck was blown up on 4 May, only four days before the German surrender.

By that time, her descendents, the modern German battleships that were to have helped turn the tide of conflict in Germany's favour, were also history.

It was in the Baltic that the first of them, the *Bismarck*, underwent her trials after completion in

ABOVE *The pre-dreadnought battleship* Schleswig-Holstein *pictured at Danzig on 10 September 1939. On 1 September 1939, she fired the opening shots of World War II against Polish positions on Westerplatte. She was severely damaged in a bombing attack on 18 December 1944 and scuttled in March 1945.*

August 1940. Built by Blohm und Voss of Hamburg, she had been launched on 14 February 1939 amid great ceremony, receiving her name from Dorothea von Löwenfeld, Bismarck's grand-daughter. Hitler and all the Nazi hierarchy had been present, at the forefront of a massive crowd.

She was truly a mighty ship. From stem to stern she measured 248m (813ft); the armour plating on her turrets and sides, made of specially hardened Wotan steel, was 33cm (13in) thick. Listed as 35,562 tonnes (35,000 tons) to comply with the London Treaty, she was in fact 42,674 tonnes (42,000 tons) standard displacement and over 50,803 tonnes (50,000) tons fully laden. With her main armament of eight 38cm (15in) guns and a speed of 54km/h (29 knots) she could outpace and outfight anything else afloat. There had never been a warship like her.

She spent 18 months fitting out, joined gradually by her key officers; men like Commander Adalbert Schneider, the gunnery commander, Captain Gerhard Junack, in charge of damage control, Commander Walter Lehmann, the chief engineer, Commander Wolf Neuendorff, the navigating officer, and Commander Hans Öls, the executive officer. Last came the captain, Ernst Lindemann, a 45-year-old Rhinelander who, everyone agreed, was admirably qualified to command such a mighty vessel.

On 24 August 1940, *Bismarck* was formally handed over and commissioned into the German Navy, and on 15

BELOW *The* Schlesien, *seen here, and the* Schleswig-Holstein *were the last pre-dreadnought battleships to serve in the German Navy.* Schlesien *saw action against Polish shore targets at the beginning of the war and also against Soviet forces in 1944–45. She was mined in the Baltic on 2 May 1945.*

September she slipped away from her Hamburg dockside and headed for the open sea. She underwent her acceptance trials in Kiel Bay, where some snags were encountered. It was not until March 1941 that the necessary modifications and adjustments were completed, enabling her to return to Kiel to complete her trials. She now sailed for Gdynia to carry out a lengthy programme of exercises and training in Danzig Bay. While this was in progress she was joined by the new 14,225-tonne (14,000-ton) heavy cruiser *Prinz Eugen*, whose captain, Helmuth Brinkmann from Lübeck, had been a classmate of Lindemann's at Naval College.

On 2 April 1941 the German Naval Staff issued preparatory orders. In the next new moon period, at the end of the month the *Bismarck*, *Prinz Eugen* and the battlecruiser *Gneisenau*, which was in Brest together with the *Scharnhorst*, were to rendezvous in the Atlantic for a combined attack on Allied shipping. *Scharnhorst* would be unable to join them because her boilers were being repaired.

Yet even without *Scharnhorst*, it was a formidable battle squadron that was preparing to put to sea. Had it done so, the results might have been disastrous for

Britain, for *Bismarck* was capable of engaging escorting warships while her two consorts attacked the convoys themselves. The carnage would have been horrendous. But on 6 April the German plans were disrupted by one of the most gallant – and in retrospect most important – deeds of the war, when Flying Officer Kenneth Campbell of No 42 Squadron RAF, at the cost of his life and those of his crew, put a torpedo into the *Gneisenau* as she lay at anchor in Brest harbour (see Chapter 3).

The German Navy C-in-C, Admiral Raeder, was now faced with a dilemma. He could postpone the sortie until *Bismarck*'s sister ship, the *Tirpitz*, was ready to join her; but she was only just about to begin her trials, and the longer the mission was delayed, the less chance there would be of the ships breaking out into the Atlantic unseen, for the northern nights would soon be short. What probably tilted the scales in favour of an immediate sortie was the fact that German forces had just invaded Greece, and any diversion that might prevent reinforcements from reaching the British Mediterranean Fleet would be valuable.

On 8 April 1941, the Task Force Commander, Admiral Günther Lütjens – who had recently been to sea with the battlecruisers – flew to Paris to confer with Admiral Karl Dönitz about co-operation between *Bismarck* and U-boats. Then, on 24 April, came a further setback; the *Prinz Eugen* was damaged by a magnetic mine, and it would take a fortnight to make repairs. Once again, Raeder was forced to consider postponement, but despite the fact that Lütjens was in favour of it – at least until *Scharnhorst* or *Tirpitz* was ready – he decided to go ahead with the sortie at the earliest opportunity.

Breakout

At the beginning of May, Lütjens flew to Gdynia (or Gotenhafen, as the Germans preferred to call it) and embarked on *Bismarck* with the officers of his staff. The forthcoming operation was allocated a codename, 'Rheinübung' ('Rhine Exercise') and a starting date of 18 May. The sortie was to be supported by a supply ship, six tankers, two patrol ships and three weather ships, deployed in the Arctic and Atlantic, while escort during the passage into the Norwegian Sea was to be provided by three destroyers and three minesweepers.

On the morning of 18 May – a Sunday – Admiral Lütjens held a final conference in his cabin, attended by his staff officers and the captains of the two warships. His operational brief from Admiral Carls of Naval Group Command North in Wilhelmshaven (who would have

shore authority over the sortie until the ships crossed the line between southern Greenland and the Hebrides, when it would come under the control of Group Command West in Paris) recommended sailing direct to Korsfjord near Bergen and remaining there for a day while the *Prinz Eugen*, whose radius of action was limited, replenished her tanks. The ships would then sail direct for the Atlantic through the Iceland-Faeroes gap. Lütjens' intention, however, was to bypass Korsfjord and proceed directly to the Arctic Ocean, refuel from the tanker *Weissenburg* near Jan Mayen Island, and then make a high-speed dash for the Atlantic through the Denmark Straits.

The hunt begins

The two warships left harbour in the afternoon and exercised until evening, when they proceeded westwards independently. At 1100 hours the next morning they made rendezvous off Arkona, the northernmost cape of Prussia, and continued with their escort of minesweepers and destroyers.

On 20 May, the force was reported in the Kattegat by the Swedish cruiser *Gotland*, and intelligence of the enemy force's northward movement reached the British Admiralty early the next day. Admiral Sir John Tovey, the C-in-C Home Fleet, at once strengthened surveillance of the northern passages into the Atlantic, ordering the battleship *Prince of Wales*, the battlecruiser *Hood* and six destroyers to sail from Scapa Flow under Vice-Admiral L.E. Holland, flying his flag in the *Hood*, while reconnaissance aircraft were despatched to search for the enemy warships. Throughout the night of 21 May, the latter steamed northwards up the Norwegian coast, following a zigzag pattern to avoid British submarines.

At 0900 hours on 22 May Lütjens had a change of mind, and ordered the task force to the Norwegian fjords after all. *Bismarck* entered Korsfjord and then Grimstadfjord, just south of Bergen, while *Prinz Eugen* went into Kalvanes Bay, to the northwest. Lütjens signalled the cruiser to take on oil from the tanker *Wollin* and to be ready to sail in the evening.

That same afternoon, the *Bismarck* and her consort were photographed by a Photographic Reconnaissance Unit Spitfire, one of two sent out to look for the ships. The Spitfire pilot, Flying Officer Michael Suckling, landed at Wick in northeast Scotland, where his film was developed; he then made a high-speed dash south with the precious prints, being forced to land at an airfield in the Midlands because of dense cloud. At 0100 hours on 22

May, having completed his journey in a fast car, Suckling who was unshaven and still wearing his flying kit, arrived at the Air Ministry in London, where he handed over the package of photographs to Air Chief Marshal Sir Frederick Bowhill, AOC-in-C Coastal Command.

Less than two hours after Suckling had walked into Bowhill's office, aircraft of Coastal Command were on their way to attack the German warships, but their operations were frustrated by bad weather. Then, shortly before nightfall on 22 May, a Martin Maryland reconnaissance aircraft of No 771 Naval Air Squadron from Hatston in the Orkneys penetrated Korsfjord and its crew, Lieutenant N.E. Goddard RNVR (pilot) and Commander G.A. Rotherham (observer) returned with the news that the *Bismarck* and *Prinz Eugen* were gone.

At 2245 hours, Admiral Tovey left Scapa Flow with the main body of the Home Fleet, heading for Icelandic waters to reinforce the heavy cruisers *Norfolk* and *Suffolk* which were patrolling the Denmark Strait. Three more cruisers were guarding Lütjens' alternative

ABOVE *The* Schleswig-Holstein *bombarding Westerplatte in September 1939. There were originally five vessels in this pre-dreadnought class of, the others being the* Deutschland, Hanover, Pommern *and* Schlesien. *The* Deutschland *was broken up in 1922, the* Hanover *in 1944–46. The* Pommern *sank in 1916.*

breakout route, between Iceland and the Faeroes. First to arrive were the Home Fleet's two fastest ships, the *Prince of Wales* and the *Hood*, which had set out in advance of the main force; behind them came Tovey's Fleet Flagship, the new battleship *King George V*, the aircraft carrier *Victorious*, four cruisers and six destroyers. The carrier was not yet fully worked up, and her air group comprised only nine Fairey Swordfish torpedo/reconnaissance aircraft and six Fairey Fulmar fighters. She had been earmarked to escort Convoy WS.8B, bound for the Middle East with troops, but had been released on Admiralty orders to take part in the hunt for the *Bismarck*. So had the battlecruiser *Repulse*, which also sailed north accompanied by three destroyers withdrawn from the Western Approaches.

At 1922 hours on 23 May, the *Bismarck* and *Prinz Eugen* were sighted by the cruiser *Suffolk* (Captain R.M. Ellis), emerging from a snow squall in the Denmark Strait. About an hour later *Suffolk* was joined by *Norfolk* (Captain A.J.L. Phillips), flying the flag of Rear-Admiral W.F. Wake-Walker, commanding the 1st Cruiser Squadron. HMS *Norfolk* came under enemy fire at a range of 11,880m (13,000 yards) and was straddled by three 38cm (15in) salvoes before retiring under cover of smoke, miraculously undamaged, to radio her enemy sighting report to Admiral Tovey, whose main fleet was still some 1110km (600nm) to the southwest. The two cruisers continued to shadow Lütjens' ships at high speed throughout the night, *Suffolk* maintaining contact with her Type 284 radar.

The *Prince of Wales* and *Hood*, meanwhile, were coming up quickly; Vice-Admiral Holland's ships had been about 408km (220nm) away at the time of the first sighting report, and Holland was anticipating a night action. His plan was to concentrate the fire of his heavy ships on the *Bismarck*, leaving Wake-Walker's cruisers to deal with the *Prinz Eugen*. What he did not know was that the *Bismarck* was no longer in the lead; the blast from her guns had put her own forward radar out of action, so Lütjens had ordered the *Prinz Eugen* to change position.

As his heavy ships approached, Admiral Holland, conscious of the need for surprise, imposed strict radio and radar silence, relying on *Suffolk*'s reports to keep him informed of the enemy's position. Soon after midnight, however, *Suffolk* lost contact, and did not regain it until 0247 hours. In the meantime Holland had turned his ships south to await full daylight, but when information

BELOW *Adolf Hitler inspecting the* Bismarck. *Hitler was fascinated by battleships and could talk with authority about their technicalities, but he knew nothing about the correct application of sea power (this would create serious problems for the navy during the war). 'On land I am a hero,' he once confessed, 'but at sea I am a coward.'*

ABOVE *The* Bismarck *in line astern, photographed from the* Prinz Eugen. *The photo was probably taken during trials in the Baltic, while the two warships were working up prior to their operational foray into the North Atlantic. It was air reconnaissance that brought the* Bismarck *to her eventual doom.*

once again began to come through from *Suffolk* he increased speed to 52km/h (28 knots) and turned on an interception course. It was now 0340 hours, and visibility was 12 miles.

At 0537 hours the opposing forces sighted each other at a range of 31km (17nm), and opened fire at 0553 hours. Both German ships concentrated their fire on the *Hood* and, thanks to their stereoscopic rangefinders, straddled her immediately; the *Bismarck*'s second and third salvoes struck the battlecruiser amidships, and those from the *Prinz Eugen* started a fire among her ready-to-use anti-aircraft ammunition. At 0600 hours, as

the British warships were altering course in order to bring all their guns to bear, the *Hood* was hit again by a salvo which pierced her lightly armoured decks and detonated in her after magazines. She blew up with a tremendous explosion and disappeared with a speed that stunned all who witnessed the event. Only three of her crew of 1419 officers and ratings survived.

As the *Prince of Wales* altered course sharply to avoid the wreckage, she herself came under heavy fire. Within moments she sustained hits by four 38cm (15in) and three 20cm (8in) shells, one of which exploded on the bridge and killed or wounded almost everyone there except her captain, J.C. Leach, who ordered the battleship to turn away under cover of smoke. The *Prince of Wales* was so newly completed that she had not yet finished working-up; the contractors were still working on her 35.5cm (14in) turrets when she sailed, and she was therefore not fully battleworthy, a fact of which Captain Leach was obviously conscious. The additional damage

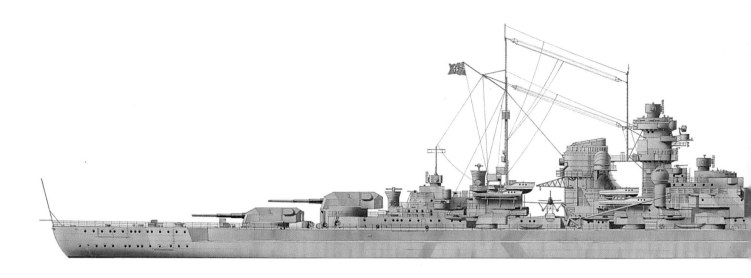

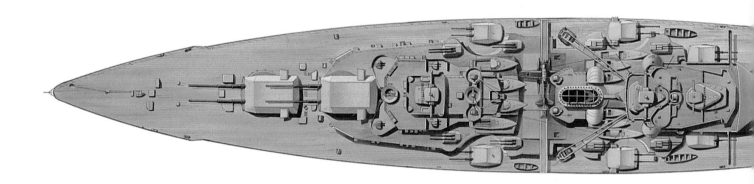

SPECIFICATIONS: *BISMARCK*

GENERAL
Ship type: Battleship
Entered service: 1940
Complement: 2400
Fate: Sunk by British fleet May 1941

MACHINERY
Engine: Diesel
Power: Three-shaft geared turbines

ARMOUR
Belt: 220–320mm (8.5–12in)
Deck: 100–120mm (3.9–4.5in)
Turrets: 360mm (14in)

ARMAMENT
Main: Eight 380mm (15in), 12 150mm
(6in) guns
Secondary: 16 105mm (4in), 16 37mm
(1.5in) AA guns

DIMENSIONS
Length: 250m (823ft 6in)
Width: 36m (118ft)
Height: 9m (29ft 6in)
Displacement: 42,370 tonnes
(41,700 tons)

PERFORMANCE
Speed: 56km/h (30 knots)

had made her even more vulnerable, and Leach's intention now was to use his damaged ship to assist Wake-Walker's cruisers in maintaining contact with the enemy until Admiral Tovey's main force could reach the scene. What Leach had no means of knowing was that his

gunners had obtained three hits on the *Bismarck*, causing two of her fuel tanks to leak oil and contaminating others, and that because of this, Lütjens had decided to abandon the sortie and steer southwest for St Nazaire, the only port on the Atlantic coast of France with a dry

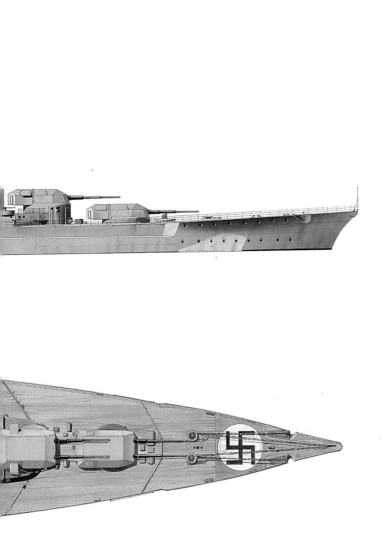

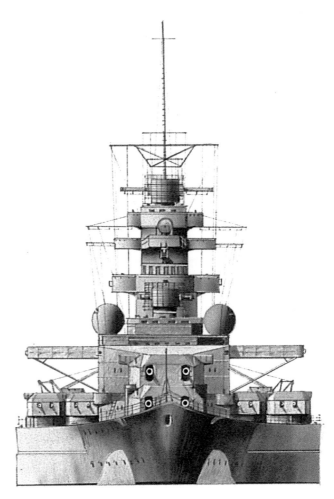

ABOVE AND LEFT *With her powerful armament and good all-over protection, the* Bismarck *was more than a match for any Allied warship, as the the British battlecruiser HMS* Hood *found out to her cost. When this superb ship was finally defeated, she took nearly 2000 of her crew of 2500 men to the bottom of the sea with her.*

dock large enough to accommodate his flagship while repairs were carried out.

Tovey's ships were still 612km (330nm) to the southeast and could not expect to make contact until 0700 hours on 25 May at the earliest. However, other ships were also heading for the scene. Admiral Somerville's Force H had been ordered north from Gibraltar by the Admiralty to intercept the German squadron, and the battleships *Rodney*, *Revenge* and *Ramillies* and the cruiser *Edinburgh* were also released from escort duties to take part in the chase. The main concern now was to reduce the *Bismarck*'s speed, giving the hunters a chance to close in for the kill, and at 1440 hours on 24 May, Admiral Tovey ordered the carrier *Victorious* to race ahead to a flying-off point 185km (100nm) from the enemy ships and launch a Swordfish strike against them.

At 2210 hours, the carrier flew off nine Swordfish of No 825 Squadron, led by Lieutenant-Commander Eugene

Esmonde. Flying through rain and sleet, they obtained radar contact with the enemy at 2337 hours and briefly sighted the *Bismarck*, only to lose her again. Twenty minutes later the shadowing British cruisers redirected the Swordfish onto their target and they made their attack through heavy defensive fire. One torpedo hit the *Bismarck* amidships without causing significant damage; the other eight missed. All the attacking Swordfish recovered safely to the carrier, although two reconnaissance Fulmars out of six despatched failed to return. The returning crews reported no sign of the *Prinz Eugen*, which had in fact been detached by Admiral Lütjens to continue on her way alone.

At 0300 hours on 25 May, Lütjens altered course to the southeast, and at this critical juncture the shadowing

cruisers, which had been following at extreme radar range, lost contact. The problems facing *Bismarck*'s pursuers were compounded by the receipt of some bearings transmitted by the Admiralty which, through a combination of errors, led Admiral Tovey to believe that the battleship was heading northeast, into the Atlantic. As a result, Tovey's flagship and many other pursuing vessels followed this false trail throughout most of 25 May, until, at about 1800 hours, he decided that the *Bismarck* was probably heading for Brest and changed course accordingly. A signal received at 1924 hours indicated that the Admiralty also thought that this was the case; in fact, the Admiralty, much earlier in the day, had already instructed Admiral Somerville's Force H to position itself on a line from which its ships and aircraft could intercept the *Bismarck* should she head for the Bay of Biscay. It turned out to be a fortuitous move.

Although Tovey's warships had lost valuable ground during their false quest to the northeast, the net around *Bismarck* was gradually closing, and it was now that the experience and tactical awareness of one man came into

ABOVE *The* Bismarck *pictured at Kiel in March 1941 having camouflage paint applied. Bright blue-white 'dazzle' camouflage was originally applied, but was substantially toned down before the battleship made her sortie into the Atlantic. Whether this camouflage made any difference to the British Navy's ability to find her is debatable.*

play. Air Chief Marshal Bowhill, who had served in the Royal Navy as a young man, persuaded his colleagues in the Admiralty that Admiral Lütjens would not steer directly for Brest, but would instead make his landfall at Cape Finisterre. Coastal Command's search aircraft were accordingly instructed to patrol well to the south, and at 1030 hours on 26, Bismarck was finally sighted nearly 1297km (700nm) west of Brest by a Catalina of No 209 Squadron from Castle Archdale (Lough Erne) in Northern Ireland. The aircraft's captain was Flying Officer Dennis Briggs, but the warship was actually sighted by his co-pilot, US Navy Ensign Leonard B. Smith, one of several US Navy pilots gaining operational experience with Coastal Command. As the USA was still ostensibly neutral, Smith's presence on the aircraft was kept a strict secret for fear of creating a diplomatic incident.

Soon after the Catalina crew sighted the *Bismarck* contact was also made by two Swordfish reconnaissance aircraft from the *Ark Royal*, Force H's aircraft carrier. Admiral Somerville sent the cruiser *Sheffield* to shadow the battleship with her Type 79Y radar and, when the opportunity arose, to direct a strike by the carrier's Swordfish torpedo-bombers. Fourteen of the latter were flown off at 1450 hours in conditions of high winds, driving rain and rough seas, and some time later their radar revealed a target which their crews assumed was the *Bismarck*. In fact it was the *Sheffield*, whose presence in the area had not been signalled to *Ark Royal*. The Swordfish came down through low cloud and attacked from different directions; several of them released their torpedoes before the mistake was recognised, but fortunately – thanks to a combination of effective evasive manoeuvring by the cruiser and faulty magnetic pistols fitted to the aircrafts' torpedoes – no damage was caused.

The vital blow

This first (and somewhat penitent) strike force returned to the carrier, which at 1910 hours launched a second wave of 15 Swordfish. The aircraft, led by Lieutenant-Commander T.P. Coode, were directed to the target by the *Sheffield*, but in the prevailing weather conditions, coupled with fading light and heavy defensive fire, they had little chance of making a co-ordinated attack. Nevertheless, two torpedoes found their mark; one struck the *Bismarck*'s armoured belt and did little damage, but the other struck her extreme stern, damaging her propellers and jamming her rudders 15 degrees to port. At 2140 hours Admiral Lütjens signalled Berlin: 'Ship no longer manoeuvrable. We fight to the last shell. Long live the Führer.'

Shortly afterwards, five destroyers, led by Captain Philip Vian in the *Cossack*, arrived on the scene, having been detached from convoy duty. They made contact with the *Bismarck* and shadowed her throughout the night, transmitting regular position reports and closing in to make a series of determined torpedo attacks, but these were disrupted by heavy and accurate radar-controlled gunfire from the German ship. Whether any torpedoes hit their target or not is still a mystery; the destroyer crews maintained that they saw two explosions on the *Bismarck*, but the survivors of the battleship later stated that no hits were made. Whatever the truth, the *Bismarck*

was seen to reduce speed, so driving a further nail into her coffin.

During the night, the battleships *Bismarck* and *Rodney* came within striking distance of their crippled enemy, but Admiral Tovey, aware of the accuracy of her radar-directed gunnery, decided to wait until daylight before engaging her; she had no means of escaping him now.

Soon after dawn on 27 May, he closed in from the northwest, his two battleships opening fire at about 0845 hours from a range of 14,600m (16,000 yards). By 1020 hours, the *Bismarck* had been reduced to a blazing wreck, with all her armament out of action, but she was still afloat despite the fact that the two British battleships had fired over 700 shells at her. Only a small proportion had found their target, prompting Admiral Tovey to tell his fleet gunnery officer that he would stand a better chance of hitting her if he threw his binoculars at her. In the end the battleships, undamaged but seriously short of fuel, were compelled to break off the action, and it was left to the cruisers *Norfolk* and *Dorsetshire* to close in and finish the *Bismarck* off with torpedoes. She sank at 1036 hours, her colours still flying, in position 48°10'N, 16°12'W, taking all but 119 of her crew of over 2000 officers and men with her. Her wreck was to lie undisturbed on the ocean floor for nearly half a century, when it was located and photographed by an underwater archaeology expedition, the swastika painted on the warship's bow still clearly visible.

Historical importance

The destruction of the Bismarck brought massive relief to the British Government. 'Had she escaped,' Winston Churchill wrote later, 'the moral effects of her continuing existence as much as the material damage she might have inflicted on our shipping would have been calamitous. Many misgivings would have arisen regarding our capacity to control the oceans, and these would have been trumpeted around the world to our great detriment and discomfort.'

The *Prinz Eugen*, meanwhile, had headed south to refuel in mid-Atlantic after parting company with the *Bismarck* on 24 May, but continuing engine defects persuaded Captain Brinkmann to abort his sortie and make for Brest. Although she was sighted by a Coastal Command patrol, she reached harbour unmolested on 1 June, aided by the fact that many British warships were in port refuelling and rearming after the pursuit of the *Bismarck*. For the rest of the year the *Prinz Eugen*,

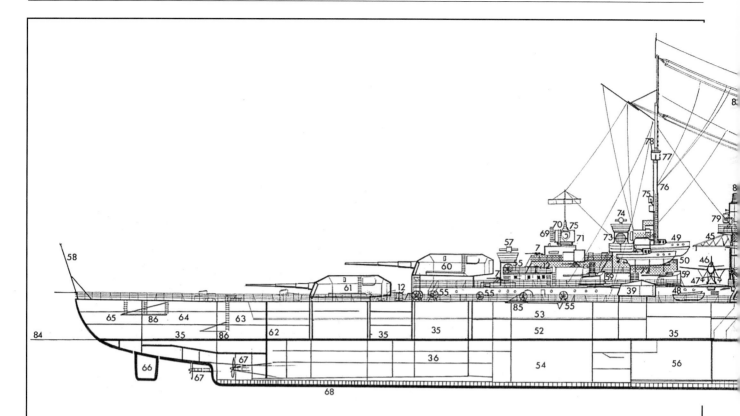

1. Radar	32. Battery deck
2. Range finder	33. Stores
3. Armoured control tower	34. Forward armoured bulkhead
4. Admirals bridge	35. Armoured or lower deck
5. Searchlight	36. Honeycomb of bulkheads
6. Day bridge	below amoured deck
7. 37mm gun	37. Barbette B turret (main arma-
8. Range finder	ment)
9. Radar	38. Machine stop
10. Gimbal-mounted AA gun	39. Barbette: secondry armament
11. AA command post	150mm (5.9in) guns
12. 20mm gun	40. Lifeboats
13. Armoured conning tower	41. Catwalk
14. Navigation room	42. Motor lifeboats
15. Wing of bridge	43. Crane
16. Turret B; 380mm (15in)	44. Funnel uptakes
17. Turret A:390-mm (15in)	45. Boat crane
guns,main armament	46. Arado 196 aircraft
18. Exhaust trunking	47. Aircraft catapult gear
19. Gunsight telescope	48. Lifeboat
20. Breech mortice	49. Motor lifeboats
21. Shell tray	50. Hanger
22. Toothed elevating gear	51. Machine shop
23. Training base on ball bearings	52. Stores
24. Elevating gear	53. Crew
25. Hydraulic pump	54. Engine gear room
26. Machinery compartment	55. Water hose reels
27. Auxiliary ammunition trunk	56. Engine and boiler rooms
28. Barbette armour	57. Anti-aircraft control
29. Rammer	58. Aft ensign mast
30. Crew quarters	59. Barbette:secondary armament
31. Anchor gear	105mm (4.1in)

60. Turret C: 380mm (15in) guns, main armament
61. Turret D: 380mm (15in) guns main armament
62. Aft armoured bulkhead
63. Winch room
64. Stores
65. Anchor gear
66. Rudder
67. Propeller shafts (3)
68. Ships double bottom
69. Radar
70. Aft superstructure
71. Armoured aft control positions
72. Boat stowage platform
73. Searchlight
74. AA control
75. Signalling lamp
76. Mainmast
77. Spotting positions
78. Rudder pointer
79. Remote control searchlight
80. Funnel
81. Searchlight-with cover in positions
82. Fore mast
83. Radio aerials
84. Waterline
85. Gangways (2)
86. Boat sponsons

BELOW *A cut-away diagram of the* Bismarck. *One Arado Ar196 spotter aircraft is shown; in fact, both* Bismarck *and* Tirpitz *had provision for six to be carried, so that reconnaissance flights could be carried out over a huge sea area during an offensive patrol.*

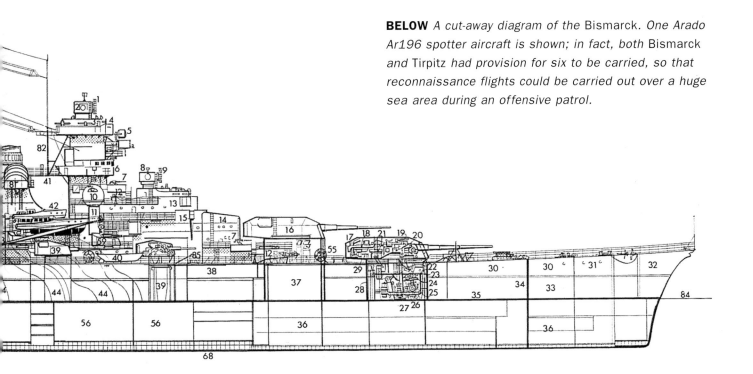

together with the battlecruisers *Scharnhorst* and *Gneisenau*, were immobilised in the Biscay ports, where they were subjected to heavy and costly attacks by RAF Bomber Command in which all three suffered damage. As a further insurance against future sorties by the enemy surface raiders, the Royal Navy began a systematic hunt for their tankers and supply ships; in June 1941, five tankers and three supply ships, plus a couple of weather observation vessels, were destroyed or scuttled after being intercepted.

For the British Admiralty, however, there remained the spectre of *Bismarck's* sister ship, the *Tirpitz*. After completion of her trials in the autumn of 1941, she was designated as flagship of the German Baltic Fleet, which was then commanded by Vice-Admiral Ciliax. In September 1941, she formed part of a battle group that sailed north to the mouth of the Gulf of Finland to counter a possible breakout into the Baltic by the Soviet Fleet; in the event this never happened, the Soviet war-ships having been subjected to fierce air attack at Kronstadt, their principal base.

Towards the end of October, British Naval Intelligence received indications that the *Tirpitz* was about to break out into the Atlantic. As an insurance against this, Admiral Tovey positioned units of the Home Fleet – the battleship *King George V*, the aircraft carrier *Victorious*, three heavy and two light cruisers – and an American battle squadron comprising the battleships *Idaho* and *Mississippi* and two cruisers south of Iceland and in the Denmark Strait. Although not yet at war with Germany, the US Navy had been participating in Atlantic convoy escort work since August 1941, following a vital meeting between Winston Churchill and US President Franklin D. Roosevelt.

It was not until the night of 16 January 1942, however, that the *Tirpitz* left her home port of Wilhelmshaven for ever, flying the flag of Vice-Admiral Ciliax and under the command of Captain Topp. Her destination was Trondheim in Norway, and the decision that she should go there on her first long voyage had been ratified by Hitler himself at a meeting with Admiral Raeder in November 1941. It was based on two considerations; the first was Hitler's concern that the British might attempt a landing in northern Norway, and the second was a shortage of fuel oil, which greatly reduced her radius of action and prevented her from being sent out on long sorties into the Atlantic. From now on the Arctic would be her hunting-ground, and the Allied convoys of supplies to the Soviet Union her quarry.

But there was also a strategic plan, outlined by Raeder at a further meeting with Hitler just before the *Tirpitz* sailed. The ship's strategic function would be to protect the German position in the Norwegian and Arctic areas by threatening the flank of enemy operations

against northern Norway, by attacking the White Sea convoys, and by tying down strong enemy forces in the Atlantic to prevent reinforcement of the Mediterranean, the Indian Ocean and the Pacific. This could be done to some degree by keeping the *Tirpitz* ready for action in Trondheim, but the best results would only be obtained by offensive sorties.

On 6 March, the *Tirpitz*, acompanied by three destroyers, set out to intercept convoys PQ12 and QP8, the first bound for Murmansk, the second on its way home. PQ12 had been detected by a FW 200 the day before, 130km (70nm) south of Jan Mayen Island, and the submarines U134, U377, U403 and U584 were also deployed to intercept it. The movements of the *Tirpitz* and her escorts, meanwhile, had been reported by the submarine Seawolf (Lieutenant Raikes). Units of the Home Fleet, comprising the battleships *King George V*, *Duke of York* and *Renown*, the carrier *Victorious*, the cruiser *Kenya* and 12 destroyers placed themselves between the threat and the convoys, which passed one another off Bear Island at noon on 7 March. Ciliax detached some of his destroyers to search for the convoys and they sank one straggling Soviet freighter, but

ABOVE: *The view from* Prinz Eugen: *a salvo from the battlecruiser HMS* Hood *bursting near the* Bismarck, *which is replying with her own guns. Moments later, the* Hood *exploded when a German shell plummeted through the deck and penetrated a magazine. There were only three survivors.*

apart from that no contact was made and the German commander turned southwards again.

Thanks to intercepted radio signals, Admiral Tovey knew of the Germans' intentions and ordered his forces towards the Lofoten Islands in an attempt to cut them off. At daybreak on 9 March, a reconnaissance Albacore from the *Victorious* spotted the *Tirpitz*, and 12 torpedo-carrying Fairey Albacores took off soon afterwards to attack the warship. The attack, unfortunately, was carried out in line astern, which gave the *Tirpitz* ample room to avoid all the torpedoes, although one passed within 30 feet of her. Two Albacores were shot down. The failure of this attack was a bitter pill for the Royal Navy to swallow, but it did have one very significant and highly advantageous result; on Hitler's orders, the *Tirpitz* never put to sea again if carrier-based aircraft were known to be in the vicinity, thus effectively neutralising her danger for most of the time.

On 11 March the battleship entered Narvik, and the following day she sailed for Trondheim, evading a force of British destroyers which tried to intercept her off Bodo. On 30 March, RAF Bomber Command mounted its first attempted attack on the warship, but the 34 Handley Page Halifax bombers sent out to Trondheim failed to locate the *Tirpitz*. One aircraft failed to return.

The British Admiralty, meanwhile, was still seriously concerned that the *Tirpitz* and other powerful surface units that were assembling in Norway might be preparing for a sortie into the Atlantic. One way of discouraging such a venture was to make it impossible for the *Tirpitz* to dock in western France, and in practice that meant putting out of action the facilities at St Nazaire, which featured the only dry dock capable of handling her. Known as the *Normandie* Lock through its association

BELOW Bismarck *seen after being hit by gunfire from the* Prince of Wales. *The damage caused the battleship to trail a telltale oil slick in her wake. Other fuel tanks were also contaminated by sea water, leaving Admiral Lütjens no alternative but to abandon his sortie and attempt a return to a friendly base.*

with the famous French passenger liner, or more correctly the Forme Ecluse, it was over 335m (1100ft) in length; and it was towards this haven that the *Bismarck* would have headed had she not been sunk in 1941.

The principal objective of the plan to raid St Nazaire, code-named Operation 'Chariot', was to ram and destroy the lock gates of the Forme Ecluse using the old ex-American destroyer HMS *Campbeltown*, her bows filled with explosives, while the destruction of the smaller South Lock gates and their installations, pumping machinery for the outer dock, and any U-boats or shipping present, were to be subsidiary objectives in that order of priority.

Combined attack

The naval force comprised the *Campbeltown* (formerly USS *Buchanan*), two escorting Hunt class destroyers, *Atherstone* and *Tynedale*, a motor gunboat, a motor torpedo boat and fifteen motor launches, four of which carried torpedoes and the remainder the military force, consisting of 44 officers and 224 other ranks of No 2 Commando and detachments from others. The naval force commander was Commander R.E.D. Ryder, RN, in peacetime an Arctic explorer and winner of the Polar Medal, while the military element of the attack force was

commanded by Lieutenant-Colonel A.C. Newman of the Essex Regiment.

The military plan of attack was based on landings at three places, from the bows of the *Campbeltown*, from motor launches on either side of the Old Entrance, and on the north side of the Old Mole. After demolition parties assigned to the three assault groups had done their work, in particular the destruction of the bridges that would effectively turn the area into an island, the force was to withdraw to the Old Mole for re-embarkation. Two hours was the maximum time allowed for the military force to complete its operation, by which time the naval force would have to leave in order to get clear before daybreak and rejoin the escorting destroyers.

The expedition sailed from Falmouth at 1400 hours on Tuesday, 26 March 1942, led by HMS *Atherstone*. The attacking force made landfall at exactly the right time and

BELOW *The* Scharnhorst *and* Gneisenau, *seen under the beginnings of a smokescreen, photographed in Brest harbour during a daylight attack by RAF Bomber Command. In 1941, Churchill directed Bomber Command to wage a four-month campaign against the warships. It cost the RAF many aircraft and crews.*

ABOVE *The old destroyer HMS* Campbeltown *firmly wedged in the Normandie Lock gates at St Nazaire, seen just before her explosives blew up and destroyed them. The damage denied the use of the Lock to the* Tirpitz, *which meant that she was debarred from operating from the French Atlantic ports.*

in the right place and succeeded in penetrating to its objective. A detailed account of the operation that followed is outside the scope of this book; suffice to say that despite bitter fighting in the harbour area it succeeded. Shortly before noon on 28 March *Campbeltown*'s demolition charges blew up with devastating effect. The lock gate, in which the destroyer's bow was jammed, was blown off its sill and seriously damaged, and the dock itself was put out of commission for the duration of the war. The cost to the British was 170 men killed or missing out of 621 committed. It was a remarkably light price to pay for the denial to the enemy of a major and threatening naval facility.

On the night of 27–28 April 1942, the *Tirpitz* was subjected to a second air attack at Trondheim, this time by 31 Halifaxes and 12 Lancasters. No hits were scored, and four Halifaxes and a Lancaster were shot down. A fifth Halifax, damaged by flak, made a forced landing on a frozen lake. The remains of this aircraft were recovered in 1982 and are now on display in the Royal Air Force Museum at Hendon, London.

On 27 June 1942, the USSR-bound convoy PQ17 sailed from Iceland with 36 freighters, protected by a close support force and a cover group of four cruisers and three destroyers. Additional long-range support was provided by a cover force from the Home Fleet, consisting of the battleships HMS *Duke of York* and USS *Washington* (the latter attached to Admiral Tovey's command), the carrier *Victorious*, two cruisers and fourteen destroyers. As soon as they learned of PQ17's departure, the German Navy initiated Operation 'Rosselsprung' ('Knight's Move'), its aim the total destruction of the convoy. In the afternoon of 2 July, Force I under Admiral Schniewind, comprising the battleship *Tirpitz* and the cruiser *Admiral Hipper*, with four destroyers and two torpedo boats, set out from Trondheim. The next day Vice-Admiral Kummetz's Force II, comprising the heavy cruisers *Lützow* and *Admiral Scheer*, with five destroyers, sailed from Narvik and headed north to join Force I at Altenfjord. There they waited, the German commanders unwilling to risk their ships until they had more information about the strength of the enemy's covering forces.

Attacks by torpedo aircraft on the convoy began on 4 July, and that evening, the Admiralty received a completely false report that a Soviet submarine had sighted the German warships heading on an interception course. This, in addition to reports that the convoy was being continually shadowed by enemy aircraft, led to one of the most tragic decisions of the war: to withdraw the escorting cruisers and destroyers and to scatter the convoy, the merchantmen making their way individually to the Soviet ports. It was the signal for packs of enemy aircraft and U-boats to fall on the hapless transports and pick them off one by one.

Death of a convoy

The slaughter began on 5 July and went on for five days, right up to the moment when the surviving ships entered Archangel. The convoy's losses were 24 ships out of 36, totalling 146,288 tonnes (143,977 tons). The losses in equipment were astronomical: 3350 vehicles, 430 tanks, 210 aircraft and 100,910 tonnes (99,316) tons of other war equipment. German losses, in over 200 sorties flown by the Luftwaffe, were just five aircraft.

Tirpitz did not sortie from Altenfjord until 5 July. She made no contact with the enemy, although she had a narrow escape when a Soviet submarine, the K21 (Captain 2nd Class Lunin) fired a salvo of torpedoes at her, which missed.

Although the *Tirpitz* remained inactive during the remainder of 1942 and the spring of 1943, the presence of the battleship and other heavy units, strategically placed in northern Norway, persuaded the Allies to suspend convoys to the Soviet Union during the Arctic summer, when the cover of darkness was stripped away. Desperate measures to eliminate the *Tirpitz* were called for. In August 1943, plans were laid to attack her with four-man midget submarines known as X-craft; these would be towed across the North Sea by specially modified submarines, make the final run to the battleship under their own power, and lay a number of explosive charges under her.

The final preparations for the attack were well under way when air reconnaissance revealed that the *Tirpitz* had left Altenfjord on 6 September. In fact, she had sailed

at the head of a task force, comprising the *Tirpitz* and nine destroyers, to bombard Allied bases on Spitzbergen. While the warships destroyed coastal batteries, the destroyers landed a battalion of the 349th Grenadier Regiment, the troops blowing up coal and supply dumps, water and electricity stations before withdrawing. It was the only occasion on which *Tirpitz*'s main armament was used in anger against a surface target.

The midget submarine attack, Operation 'Source', finally got under way on 21 September 1943, after it was confirmed that the enemy warships had returned to Altenfjord. Two of the small craft, X8 and X9, were lost in passage; X5 was never heard from again, probably destroyed while passing through a minefield; and X10 had to abandon the sortie after breaking down. Only X6 (Lieutenant D. Cameron RNVR) and X7 (Lieutenant B.G.C. Place RN) succeeded in penetrating into the anchorage to lay their charges under the *Tirpitz*. Cameron then scuttled his craft, he and his crew being picked up and taken on board the battleship; Place tried to force his way back through the torpedo nets surrounding the *Tirpitz*, but was still entangled when the charges detonated, sending X7 out of control. Place and one other crew member got clear, but the other two were lost when the craft sank.

The charges exploded at 0812 hours on 22 September, the log of the *Tirpitz* recording: 'Two heavy consecutive detonations to port at a tenth of a second interval. Ship vibrates strongly in vertical direction, and sways slightly between the anchors.' The ship seemed to rise several feet out of the water and fell back with a slight list. All the lights went out, watertight doors jammed, gear of all sorts broke loose, and general uproar ensued. The damage was substantial. One of the turbines had been shaken from its bed, and 'C' turret, which weighed about 2032 tonnes (2000 tons), had been lifted by the force of the explosion (which had occurred directly underneath it), from off the roller path of ball bearings on which it rested, dropped down again and jammed. In addition, all the rangefinders and fire control gear had been put out of action. Everything but the turret could be repaired on the spot, but it would take a long time. In fact, it would take until March 1944.

Out of action

For her repairs, *Tirpitz* retreated into Kaafjord, a narrow body of water leading off Altenfjord. The berth had been selected earlier, as the high, steep mountains on both sides of the fjord made air attack very difficult, especially

ABOVE *The German Northern Battle Squadron leaving a Norwegian port (probably Altenfjord) in the summer of 1942. The scene is photographed from the* Tirpitz; *the next ship astern is the heavy cruiser* Admiral Hipper, *followed by the* Admiral Scheer, *with their escorting destroyers visible in the background.*

for torpedo-bombers. On the night of 10-11 February 1944, however, 15 Ilyushin Il-4 bombers of the Soviet Naval Air Arm, each carrying a 1000kg (2250lb) bomb, set out to attack the battleship. Four of the Soviet crews found their target, and one bomb registered a near miss, causing slight damage.

In a bid to knock the *Tirpitz* out once and for all, before she could be made fully seaworthy again, the C-in-C Home Fleet (now Admiral Sir Bruce Fraser) planned a massive Fleet Air Arm strike against her. To simulate her anchorage in Altenfjord, a dummy range was built on

Loch Eriboll, in Caithness, Scotland, and during March 1944 this was the scene of intense activity as aircraft from the *Victorious* and *Furious* rehearsed the attack plan.

The strike was to be carried out by the 8th and 52nd TBR (Torpedo Bomber Reconnaissance) Wings, operating the Fairey Barracuda, a type that had first seen action during the Salerno landings in Italy eight months earlier. In addition to their TBR Wings, the *Victorious* and *Furious* also carried Nos 1834 and 1836 Squadrons, equipped with American-built Vought Corsair fighters, and Nos 801 and 880 Squadrons with Seafires. More fighter cover was to be provided by the Hellcats of Nos 800 and 804 Squadrons (HMS *Emperor*) and the Martlet Vs of Nos 861, 896, 882 and 898 Squadrons (HMS *Pursuer* and *Searcher*), while anti-submarine patrols were to be flown by the Swordfish of 842 Squadron on board HMS *Fencer*. The carrier group was to be covered by warships of the

SPECIFICATIONS: *TIRPITZ*

GENERAL

Ship type: Battleship

Entered service: 1941

Complement: 2400

Fate: Sunk by British bombers

MACHINERY

Engine: Diesel

Power: Three screws, Brown-Boveri geared turbines, 12 Wagner boilers

ARMOUR

Belt: 220–320mm (8.5–12in)

Deck: 100–120mm (3.9–4.5in)

Turrets: 360mm (14in)

ARMAMENT

Main: Eight 380mm (15in), 12 150mm (6in) guns

Secondary: 16 105mm (4in), 16 37mm (1.5in) AA guns

DIMENSIONS

Length: 248m (813ft 6in)

Width: 36m (118ft)

Height: 10.2m (33ft 9in)

Displacement: 43,588 tonnes (42,900 tons)

PERFORMANCE

Speed: 59km/h (32 knots)

Home Fleet, consisting of the battleships *Duke of York* and *Anson*, the cruisers *Belfast*, *Jamaica*, *Royalist* and *Sheffield* and 14 destroyers, and the strike was timed to coincide with the passage of a Soviet convoy, JW58.

On 30 March 1944, the Home Fleet units sailed from Scapa Flow in two forces, the first comprising the two battleships, the *Victorious*, one cruiser and five destroyers, and the second of the *Furious*, the four escort carriers and three cruisers. The actual attack on the *Tirpitz*, code-named Operation 'Tungsten', was to be conducted by Vice-Admiral Sir Henry Moore, second-in-command of the Home Fleet, flying his flag in the *Anson*.

The forces assembled in the afternoon of 2 April, about 350km (220nm) to the northwest of Altenfjord and

from there moved to the flying-off position, 222km (120nm) northwest of Kaafjord, reaching it during the early hours of the following morning. At 0430 hours, 21 Barracudas of No 8 TBR Wing, escorted by 21 Corsairs and 20 Hellcats, took off from the *Victorious* and set course for the target. Fifty miles from their objective, the Barracudas, which had been flying low over the sea to avoid radar detection, went up to 2440m (8000ft) and began their final approach, preceded by the fighters which went in at low level to suppress flak. The Germans were taken by surprise and the *Tirpitz*, lying virtually naked under the beginnings of a smoke screen, was hit by nine armour-piercing or semi-armour-piercing bombs. An hour later, a second attack was made by 19 Barracudas

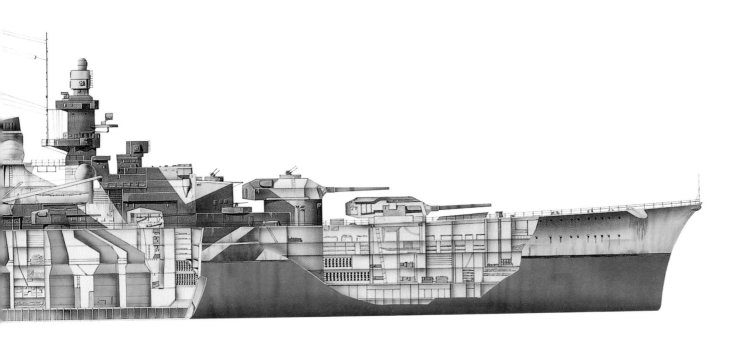

ABOVE *Cut-away diagram of the battleship* Tirpitz. *With several capital ships like the* Tirpitz *and* Bismarck, *supported by aircraft carriers, the whole operating in conjunction with U-boat packs, Germany would almost certainly have gained command of the Atlantic.*

BELOW *An Atlantic convoy assembling off Halifax, Nova Scotia. Convoys became much better protected after America's entry into the war. Ultra intelligence often enabled them to be routed around the U-boat packs and long range patrol aircraft gave additional protection.*

of No 52 TBR Wing, escorted by 39 fighters, and the performance was repeated. By this time the smoke screen was fully developed, but it hindered the German gunners far more than it did the Barracuda crews, who had no difficulty in locating their target. In all, the battleship was hit by 14 bombs, 122 of her crew being killed and 316 wounded; although the bombs failed to penetrate her heavy armour, they caused extensive damage to her superstructure and fire control systems and put her out of action for a further three months. The British lost two Barracudas and a Hellcat.

Further attempts to attack the *Tirpitz* in May were frustrated by bad weather, the naval aircraft instead turning their attention to enemy convoys off the Norwegian coast and scoring some successes. It was not until 17 July 1944 that another raid was carried out, this time by aircraft from the *Formidable*, *Furious* and *Indefatigable* under the command of Rear-Admiral R.R. McGrigor. The covering force, comprising the battleship *Duke of York*,

the cruisers *Bellona*, *Devonshire*, *Jamaica* and *Kent*, was commanded by Admiral Sir Henry Moore, now C-in-C Home Fleet in place of Admiral Sir Bruce Fraser. Forty-five Barracudas of Nos 820 and 826 Squadrons (*Indefatigable*) and 827 and 830 Squadrons (*Formidable*) set out to make the attack; the 50-strong fighter escort included the Fairey Fireflies of No 1770 Squadron, seeing combat for the first time. However, the enemy had plenty of warning. A smoke screen and alert anti-aircraft defences made the raid unsuccessful.

The next attack, carried out on 22 August, was a disaster; the incoming aircraft were detected a long way

BELOW AND RIGHT *The* Tirpitz *photographed at anchor in Kaafjord and Narvikfjord by a reconnaissance Spitfire in 1942. The protective anti-torpedo nets are clearly visible. Despite such precautions, the battleship was badly damaged by a midget submarine attack in September 1943, effectively ending her war.*

from the target and were intercepted by Me 109s of JG5, the Luftwaffe's 'Arctic Wing', which shot down 11 of them, mostly Barracudas. The escort carrier *Nabob* was torpedoed off North Cape by the U534 and damaged beyond repair; the U534 was herself sunk by aircraft from the escort carrier *Vindex* three days later. Two minor bomb hits were obtained on the *Tirpitz* in an attack on 24 August, the Barracuda crews bombing blind through the smoke, and a further attack, on 29 August, was unsuccessful. Counting a mission that had to be aborted because of the weather on 20 August, the Fleet Air Arm flew 247 sorties in this series of attacks.

RAF Bomber Command, meanwhile, had recently begun to attack precision targets with its latest weapon, the 5443kg (12,000lb) 'Tallboy' deep-penetration bomb,

and in August 1944, No 5 Bomber Group, which had pioneered the weapon into service, was instructed to assess the feasibility of using it to destroy the *Tirpitz*. It was the only bomb in existence capable of penetrating the battleship's two layers of deck armour, the upper layer being 100mm (3.93in) and the lower one 120mm (4.7in) thick.

Range was a principal problem; Kaafjord lay 2224km (1200nm) from the nearest British airfield, beyond the capability of the Lancaster bombers that carried the Tallboy. To overcome this, agreement was reached with the Russians that the Lancasters of Nos 9 and 617 Squadrons – the specialist 'Tallboy' squadrons – would strike at the *Tirpitz* from the Soviet airfield of Yagodnik, on the Archangel peninsula. After a great deal of planning

and organisation, 38 Lancasters of the two squadrons set out for North Russia on the evening of 11 September 1944. Of this force, which encountered appalling weather en route, one aircraft aborted and returned to Britain when its Tallboy bomb broke loose and had to be jettisoned, six more crash-landed in Russia and had to be abandoned, and two were immediately placed unfit for operations on arrival at Yagodnik. Two Liberators carrying the ground crews arrived safely, as did a weather reconnaissance Mosquito and a Lancaster carrying an RAF film unit.

On 15 September, 27 Lancasters, plus the film unit aircraft, took off from Yagodnik to attack the battleship. No problem was envisaged with the weather, for the reconnaissance Mosquito had surveyed the bombers' route earlier and had reported that conditions were favourable. The main obstacle to the success of the mission was likely to be the massive defensive smokescreen which the Germans were known to be capable of laying across the *Tirpitz*'s anchorage for a very short time.

The plan called for the bombers to attack in two waves. The first, consisting of 21 Lancasters carrying Tallboys, was to bomb from between 4270 and 5490m (14,000 and 18,000ft), while behind them at between 3050 and 6660m (10,000 and 12,000ft) came six more Lancasters carrying 225kg (500lb) 'Johnny Walker' mines, specially developed for attacking vessels moored in shallow water. Initially the whole force was to make its approach at 300m (1000ft) to achieve the maximum element of surprise. This height was to be maintained until the Finnish border was reached, when the bombers were to climb to between 610 and 915m (2000 and 3000ft) above their bombing height. This would enable them to make their

bombing run in a shallow dive, affording the extra speed that would be vital if the bombs were to be released before the enemy smokescreen had time to form.

Apart from a major course alteration made necessary by the Tallboy-armed Lancasters straying off track (their compasses were made unreliable by the large iron ore deposits in the mountains), the flight to the target was uneventful. As they approached the fjord in an almost cloudless sky the crews had a clear view of the battleship. Then the smokescreen began to form and she was quickly obscured, but five Tallboys went down in her immediate vicinity during the next 60 seconds. The crews that followed took the battleship's flak bursts as their aiming point, and some felt sure that more than one hit had been obtained. There was, however, no way of obtaining any confirmation at this stage, for as the Lancasters left the target area the whole fjord lay under a dense blanket of smoke. Post-raid reconnaissance was also frustrated by cloud, which began to creep across the sky soon after the attack, and when the reconnaissance Mosquito arrived over Altenfjord some two hours later its

BELOW *Fairey Barracuda dive-bombers of the Fleet Air Arm setting out to attack the* Tirpitz *in April 1944. Fourteen bombs hit the battleship during the attack, causing enough damage to immobilise her until she could be sunk at a later date by heavy bombs from RAF Bomber Command.*

crew got only the briefest glimpse of the vessel through a gap in the clouds.

In fact the *Tirpitz* had been damaged to a far greater extent than any of the attacking crews dreamed. One Tallboy had gone straight through her overhanging bow and exploded in the water, the force of the explosion wrecking the deck plating as far as the forward turret and causing further damage to her main engine frames. It was estimated that even if she could reach a north German shipyard with full repair facilities, it would be at least nine months before she could be made battleworthy again. The Germans, however, declined to risk the battleship in a slow voyage down the Norwegian coast; at six or seven knots, the best speed she could make with her damaged engines, she would be a sitting target. Instead they sent her to a new anchorage at Tromso, from where it was planned that her heavy armament would help repel an Allied invasion of northern Norway. She was protected from underwater attack by a double net barrage, and from air attack by smokescreens, anti-aircraft batteries on the shore and two flak ships, *Nymph* and *Thetis*.

The British Admiralty had at this stage no way of knowing that the *Tirpitz*'s fighting days were over. As far as naval intelligence was concerned, Tromso might simply be a staging point for some other destination. At any rate the warship was still afloat, and as such she

continued to present a threat. By 24 October, another plan had been devised for an attack on the battleship in her new anchorage, and Nos 9 and 617 Squadrons were once more working out the details of the operation.

This time, since Tromso was some 370km (200nm) closer to the British Isles than Altenfjord, it was decided to launch the attack from a home base: Lossiemouth, in Scotland. The round trip involved a flight of 4170km (2250nm), so to compensate for the weight of the Tallboys and the extra fuel that would have to be carried the Lancasters were stripped of all equipment, including mid-upper gun turrets, that was not considered absolutely necessary. The front guns and ammunition, oxygen bottles and armour plating were all removed. Since no enemy fighters had been encountered during the previous attack the elimination of most of the Lancasters' firepower seemed a justifiable risk, and as all the flight with the exception of the attack phase was to be flown at 610m (2000ft) the oxygen would not be missed. Even

BELOW *The Fleet Air Arm attack of 3 April 1944 took the German defences by surprise. Here, smoke generators on the shore of Altenfjord are just beginning to put up a protective screen as the first wave as the attack goes in. The battleship has raised steam and is about to move to present a more difficult target.*

ABOVE *The Fleet Air Arm's bombs bursting on and around the* Tirpitz. *The successful attack of 3 April 1944 demonstrated the value of the dive-bomber against stationary or near-stationary vessels; the light cruiser* Königsberg *had been sunk by the Fleet Air Arm in this way in April 1940.*

with all these weight-saving precautions the bombers' fuel would be marginal, and pilots were told that any Lancaster with less than 4,090 litres (900 gallons) remaining after the attack was to carry on to the Soviet Union and land at Yagodnik or Vaenga.

On the morning of 20 October, the strike force was ready. It consisted of 18 Lancasters of No 617 Squadron and 18 of No 9, led respectively by Wing Commanders J.B. Tait and J.M. Bazin. The aircraft took off in pouring rain and reached the target area at 0900 hours. The crews had a clear view of the *Tirpitz* as they began their run-in, but at the very last moment – 30 seconds before the first Lancaster was ready to bomb – low cloud drifted in from the sea and obscured the anchorage. Thirty-three aircraft attacked through heavy flak and dropped their Tallboys,

aiming through partial gaps in the cloud, but they were able to claim only one near miss. One aircraft was damaged by flak and force-landed in Sweden.

For 12 days, the two squadrons stood by, waiting for a favourable opportunity to strike at the battleship once more. At 0200 hours on 12 November 1944, 30 Lancasters again set out from Lossiemouth, making landfall on the Norwegian close in brilliantly clear weather. At a distance of 20 miles the crews sighted the *Tirpitz*. There was no cloud, no smokescreen. Like a great spider nestling in a web of anti-submarine booms, the battleship lay naked.

The *Tirpitz* opened fire, and soon she was obscured by the smoke of her massive defensive armament. The Lancasters continued their bombing runs through countless shellbursts flung up by the battleship, the two flak ships and the shore batteries, and at 0940 hours Wing Commander Tait released the first Tallboy. More bombs went down as Tait dived away to port, exploding on or around the battleship, raising immense columns of smoke and water. As Tait and his crew watched, a column of steam shot up to a height of 100m (330ft), penetrating

the darker clouds of gun smoke that shrouded the warship.

Following the main force came a Lancaster of No 463 Squadron, filming the attack. As it ran overhead, its crew saw the battleship slowly capsize, torn apart by two direct hits and a massive internal explosion. When a Mosquito photographed the scene two hours later, the *Tirpitz* had almost completely turned turtle in the shallow waters of the fjord, her superstructure resting on the bottom.

Twenty-eight officers, including the *Tirpitz*'s latest commander, Captain Weber, and 874 crewmen perished with the ship; 880 were rescued. The cost to the RAF was one Lancaster, which came down in Sweden with flak damage, its crew unharmed.

The remains of the *Tirpitz*, with the bodies of many of her crew still trapped inside, lay in her last resting place for a dozen years, being cut up slowly piece by piece, her rusting hulk a testament to Nazi Germany's

ABOVE *The end of the* Tirpitz. *Attacked by Lancaster bombers of Nos 9 and 617 Squadrons on 12 November 1944, she was hit by two 4725kg (12,000lb) bombs and capsized with heavy loss of life. Both squadrons claimed to have dropped the bomb that sank the ship, beginning a friendly rivalry that lasts to this day.*

RIGHT *British personnel inspecting the upturned hulk of the* Tirpitz *after the end of the war. The process of cutting up the battleship went on for several years and was a rather gruesome business, for bodies entombed in the hull were still being recovered long after the vessel was sunk.*

vain hopes of gaining dominion of the seas. That neither the *Tirpitz*, nor the *Bismarck,* achieved their full deadly potential was a tribute to the skill, tenacity and, most importantly, the good fortune of the Allied navies – but it was a close run thing at the time.

CHAPTER 3

THE SCHARNHORST AND GNEISENAU

In the early years of World War II, the powerful battlecruisers *Scharnhorst* and *Gneisenau* remained a constant thorn in the side of the British Admiralty. In February 1942, they dealt a severe blow to British pride when they made their famous dash through the English Channel, homeward bound for Germany.

When the German Navy went to war in September 1939, its most powerful and potentially most destructive warships were the battlecruisers *Scharnhorst* and *Gneisenau*. From the very beginning they were priority targets for the bombers of the Royal Air Force; on 4 September, the

LEFT *The German Navy's Commander Battleships, Vice-Admiral Ciliax, inspecting the crew of the* Scharnhorst, *accompanied by Captain Hoffman (right) and executive officers. Together, the* Scharnhorst, Gneisenau *and* Prinz Eugen *made a formidable battle unit.*

second day, they were unsuccessfully attacked by 14 Vickers Wellingtons at Brunsbüttel, two aircraft being shot down by fighters.

On 7 October the *Gneisenau*, accompanied by the light cruiser *Köln* and nine destroyers, made a brief sortie towards the south coast of Norway, attempting to draw units of the British Home Fleet into contact with a screen of U-boats and within range of German bombers. Both sides were subjected to air attacks, but without result. The *Gneisenau* returned to port on 9 October.

On 21 November, the *Scharnhorst* (Captain Hoffmann) and *Gneisenau* (Captain Förste) sailed from

ABOVE *Photograph of the* Gneisenau's *forward 28cm (11in) armament. The German battlecruisers could be outgunned by British battleships, but against enemies with lesser firepower, they were deadly, as shown by the sinking of the aircraft carrier* Glorious *in June 1940.*

BELOW *The* Gneisenau *was the second battlecruiser to bear that name, the first having been sunk by British cruisers at Jutland in 1916. During the 'Channel Dash' of 1942, she was badly damaged by a mine; eventually her turrets were removed to use as shore defences.*

Wilhelmshaven for the North Atlantic, the purpose of their sortie being to divert attention away from the operations of the pocket battleship *Admiral Graf Spee* in the South Atlantic. Passing undetected to the north of the Shetlands and Faeroes, the warships were sighted on 23 November by the Armed Merchant Cruiser *Rawalpindi* (Captain E.C. Kennedy), which engaged them in a gallant but one-sided duel and had time to radio their presence to Scapa Flow before she was sunk by the *Scharnhorst*. Admiral Sir Charles Forbes, the C-in-C Home Fleet, at once ordered the entire Home Fleet to sea in a bid to intercept the battlecruisers. They were in fact sighted by the cruiser *Newcastle*, which had been patrolling in the vicinity, as they were in the process of picking up survivors from the *Rawalpindi*, but they avoided her in a

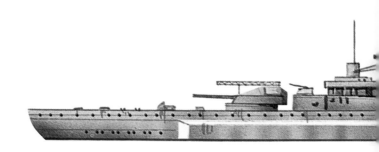

rain squall and withdrew to a waiting position inside the Arctic Circle.

On 26 November, the battlecruisers came south once more, passed through the cruiser and destroyer patrol lines which Admiral Forbes had established off Norway, and regained Wilhelmshaven the next day. No fewer than 60 warships – six battleships (three French), two battle-cruisers, 20 cruisers (two French), 28 destroyers (eight French), three submarines and an aircraft carrier – had been redeployed to various positions in the North Atlantic and North Sea to hunt the *Scharnhorst* and *Gneisenau*, and the Germans had eluded the lot. As a diversionary tactic, it had certainly worked.

The two battlecruisers were again at sea on 18 February 1940, taking part in Operation 'Nordmark', an attempt to intercept British convoy traffic in the Shetland-Norway gap. They were unsuccessful, and returned to Wilhelmshaven to prepare for a much greater undertaking. On 9 April 1940, the period that had become known as the 'Phoney War' came to a violent end when German forces invaded Norway and Denmark. The decision to occupy Norway was not entirely to do with securing the vital iron ore route; the German naval C-in-C, Admiral Erich Raeder, had learned an important lesson from history, or rather from a book published in 1929, entitled Maritime Strategy of the Great War. Its author, Vice-Admiral Wegener, had pointed out that if Germany had occupied Norway in 1914, the High Seas Fleet, using Norwegian harbours, would have been free to operate against Britain's North Atlantic convoys instead of remaining blockaded in the North German ports by the Royal Navy's Home Fleet based at Scapa Flow.

There had been plenty of warning of Germany's intention to invade Norway. Early in April, the British Government had received intelligence reports of unusual German activity in the Baltic ports, and interpreted this as a sign that the German Fleet was preparing to break out into the Atlantic. This interpretation was wrong.

SPECIFICATIONS: *GNEISENAU*

GENERAL
Ship type: Battlecruiser
Entered service: 1938
Complement: 1800
Fate: Sunk as a blockship in 1945

MACHINERY
Engine: Diesel
Power: Three screws, geared turbines

ARMOUR
Belt: 70–350mm (2.7–13.6in)
Deck: 50–105mm (2–4in)
Turrets: 150–360mm (5.8–14in)

ARMAMENT
Main: Nine 280mm (11in), 12 150mm (6in) guns
Secondary: 14 105mm (4in), 16 37mm (1.5in) AA guns; six 53cm (21in) torpedo tubes

DIMENSIONS
Length: 229.8m (754ft)
Width: 30m (98ft 6in)
Height: 9.9m (32ft 6in)
Displacement: 32,514 tonnes (32,000 tons)

PERFORMANCE
Speed: 57km/h (31 knots)

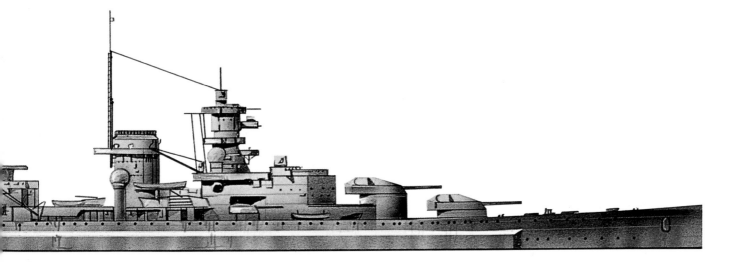

RIGHT Gneisenau, *seen after modification in 1939, with lengthened bow. She and her sister ship, Scharnhorst, had a successful time against Allied shipping, sinking 24 vessels during their combined foray into the Atlantic in February and March 1941, in addition to the* Rawalpindi *and the carrier* Glorious.

The bulk of the enemy invasion force was already at sea on 7 April, steaming northwards through savage weather. This part of the invasion force was divided into three Task Groups. Group One, with Narvik as its objective, had the farthest distance to travel – roughly 1850km (1000nm) – and was heavily escorted by the battlecruisers *Scharnhorst* and *Gneisenau*, together with 10 destroyers. In the evening of 8 April, the British Admiralty instructed Admiral Forbes that his primary objective was the interception of the *Scharnhorst* and *Gneisenau*, still in the belief that a breakout into the Atlantic was in the offing.

It was not until 1900 hours on 8 April that the Admiralty, following an assessment of further intelligence reports on the movements of German vessels, decided that an invasion was under way - although the possibility of a simultaneous breakout into the Atlantic was not discounted. A signal was flashed to the commander of the northermost group of British warships, Vice-Admiral William Whitworth, in HMS *Renown*.

'Most immediate. The force under your orders is to concentrate on preventing any German force proceeding to Narvik.'

It was too late. Before midnight, the German invasion forces were already entering the fjords that led to their objectives. At 0337 hours on 9 April, however, *Renown*, positioned 50 miles off the entrance to Vestfjord, sighted the *Scharnhorst* and *Gneisenau*, heading northwest to prevent any British interference with the Narvik assault group. Mistaking one of them for the cruiser *Hipper*, the British battlecruiser opened fire at 17,290m (19,000 yards) and got three heavy hits on the *Gneisenau*. The German warships returned fire with their 18 28cm (11in) guns, hitting *Renown* twice but causing little damage, and then turned away to the northeast; the German commander, Admiral Günther Lütjens, had decided not to take unnecessary risks against what he believed to be the battleship *Repulse*. It was lucky for the *Renown* that one of her shells put the *Gneisenau*'s Seetakt ranging radar and its associated gunnery control system out of action.

The two battlecruisers, their escort mission successfully accomplished, returned to Wilhelmshaven to undergo an extensive overhaul (and, in the case of *Gneisenau*, repair work) that lasted six weeks. They did not make another sortie until the closing stages of the Norwegian Campaign in June 1940, when they set out as part of a task group with orders to attack Allied transport convoys evacuating troops from northern Norway.

Two major British warships proceeded independently of the convoys on 7 June. One was the cruiser *Devonshire*, sailing for Scapa Flow with King Haakon of Norway and members of his government; the other was

the carrier *Glorious*, homeward bound at reduced speed because she was short of fuel. She carried Gloster Gladiator and Hawker Hurricane fighters, the survivors of two RAF squadrons that had fought in Norway, together with their personnel. The carrier was escorted only by the destroyers *Ardent* and *Acasta*.

On the afternoon of 8 June, *Glorious* and her escorts were intercepted by the *Scharnhorst* and *Gneisenau*, searching for Allied troop transports west of Harstad. The carrier was caught completely unaware; for reasons that were never explained, none of her reconnaissance Swordfish were airborne. Desperate attempts were made

to arm and launch them as the enemy battlecruisers came in sight, but she was overwhelmed and sunk before this could be accomplished. Her escorting destroyers were also sunk, but not before the *Acasta*, already doomed, had hit the *Scharnhorst* with a torpedo. The warship limped into Trondheim, and on 13 June the *Ark Royal* flew off a strike of 15 Skuas of Nos 800 and 803 Squadrons against her. One 225kg (500lb) bomb hit the battlecruiser and failed to explode; eight Skuas failed to return.

On 21 June, a reconnaissance Sunderland flying boat reported that the *Scharnhorst* had left Trondheim and was steaming slowly south escorted by eight destroyers

and torpedo boats. Attacks by RAF Beaufort torpedo-bombers and by Fleet Air Arm Swordfish were beaten off, the attackers suffering heavy losses, and the *Scharnhorst* reached Kiel on 23 June without further damage. The important fact, though, was that *Acasta*'s torpedo hit had almost certainly averted the destruction of the Allied convoys which were the German warships' main objectives.

On 20 June, to divert attention from the damaged *Scharnhorst*, the *Gneisenau* left Trondheim to make a sortie into the Iceland-Faeroes passage. She was sighted 74km (40nm) northwest of Halten by the British submarine *Clyde*, whose commander, Lieutenant-Commander Ingram, obtained a torpedo hit on *Gneisenau*'s bow. The warship recovered to Trondheim, and after temporary repairs sailed for Kiel on 25 July, arriving two days later.

The *Scharnhorst* (Captain Hoffmann) and *Gneisenau* (Captain Fein) did not leave their north German refuge again until 28 December 1940, when they attempted to break out into the North Atlantic to attack merchant shipping. However, on 2 January 1941, off

ABOVE Gneisenau *in action against the aircraft carrier* Glorious *on 8 June 1940.* Glorious *was sunk with the loss of about 800 lives, including most of the pilots of the two fighter squadrons she was evacuating from Norway. For some reason, the carrier's Swordfish torpedo bombers were not launched.*

Norway, the *Gneisenau* suffered severe storm damage and the sortie was abandoned on the orders of the force commander, Admiral Lütjens. Their next attempt (Operation 'Berlin') began on 22 January, when they left Kiel. They were sighted the following day, and the British Home Fleet, now commanded by Admiral Tovey, set out to intercept them south of Iceland. Patrolling cruisers sighted them as they tried to break through, but contact was broken and the German warships withdrew into the Arctic for replenishment. On the night of 3–4 February 1941, they passed through the Denmark Strait undetected.

On 8 February, in the North Atlantic, they sighted the British Convoy HX106 east of Newfoundland, but Lütjens thought it prudent not to attack as the merchantmen were escorted by the battleship *Ramillies*. On 22 February, however, still about 925km (500nm) east of Newfoundland, they fell upon a westbound convoy which had dispersed and sank five ships totalling 26,198 tonnes (25,784 tons).

On Saturday, 15 March 1941 the two warships were operating in the central North Atlantic when they encountered the scattered ships of another dispersed convoy. The result was a massacre. The *Gneisenau* sank seven freighters totalling 27,122 tonnes (26,693 tons) and captured three tankers of 20,462 tonnes (20,139 tons), while the *Scharnhorst* sank six ships totalling 35,562 tonnes (35,080 tons).

Gneisenau, however, had an extremely narrow escape; as she was picking up survivors from her last victim, she was surprised by the battleship HMS *Rodney*, whose captain had been alerted by a distress call and had detached his ship from Convoy XH114 and rushed to the scene. Captain Fein, making good use of the *Gneisenau*'s superior speed and manoeuvrability, managed to avoid an engagement with his more heavily armed opponent, and slipped away, before the British

warship was able to engage him in combat and bring to bear its powerful guns.

The British Admiralty immediately launched a major operation to trap the German warships, sending the battleships *Rodney* and *King George V* north, to join a third battleship, HMS *Nelson*, a cruiser and two destroyers in covering the Iceland passages. Meanwhile, Force H, with the battlecruiser Renown, the aircraft carrier *Ark Royal*, the cruiser *Sheffield* and some destroyers, set out from Gibraltar to cover the approaches to the French Atlantic ports, and on 20 March a Swordfish reconnaissance aircraft from the carrier sighted the tankers captured by the *Gneisenau*. With Force H coming up fast the prize crews were forced to scuttle two of the vessels, but the third managed to evade the British warships and reached the Gironde estuary. The

BELOW *The* Scharnhorst *in the Atlantic during the sortie against British convoys in 1941. The photograph clearly shows her Arado Ar196 reconnaissance aircraft, suspended above the deck, which was issued to all the German capital ships and was operated by the ship-based Bordfliegergruppe 5/BFGr 196.*

two German battlecruisers were also sighted by a Swordfish later in the day, but the aircraft had radio trouble and by the time its report was transmitted, the warships had slipped away. On 22 March they were met by the torpedo boats *Iltis* and *Jaguar* and escorted into Brest. Their sortie had cost the Allies 22 ships totalling 117,478 tonnes (115,622 tons).

Photographic reconnaissance did not detect the German warships at Brest until 28 March, and as soon as he learned of it, Winston Churchill issued a directive that the battlecruisers were to become a primary target for RAF Bomber Command. The air offensive began on the night of 30-31 March, when 109 aircraft were despatched to attack Brest harbour without result. There was a further abortive attack on 4-5 April by 54 aircraft; their bombs caused considerable damage to the town and one fell in the dry dock alongside the *Gneisenau* without exploding. Captain Fein thought it advisable to move the ship to the outer harbour, where she would be safer if the bomb detonated while it was being disarmed.

She was located by a photo-reconnaissance Spitfire, and a strike by Coastal Command aircraft was arranged.

ABOVE *The dramatic painting by Norman Wilkinson depicting the fatal encounter between the* Scharnhorst *and the* Rawalpindi, *southeast of Iceland, on 23 November 1939. All 15 of the fast merchant ships which the British converted to the armed cruiser role at the beginning of the war were sunk.*

The sortie was flown at dawn on 6 April 1941 by six Bristol Beauforts of No 22 Squadron from St Eval, in Cornwall, but only one succeeded in locating the target in bad visibility. The pilot of this particular aircraft, Flying Officer Kenneth Campbell, made his torpedo run at mast height through intense flak put up by more than 250 guns around the anchorage, as well as by three flak ships and the *Gneisenau*'s own armament. The Beaufort was eventually brought down by this massive defensive effort, with the loss of all its crew, but not before Campbell had released his torpedo at a range of 450m (490 yards). The torpedo exploded on the *Gneisenau*'s stern below the waterline, putting the cruiser out of action for months. For his gallant action, Campbell was posthumously awarded the Victoria Cross. The other members of his crew were Sergeant J.P. Scott, Sergeant W. Mullis and Sergeant R.W. Hillman.

The *Gneisenau* was further damaged by Bomber Command on the night of 10–11 April 1941, when she was hit by four bombs; 50 Germans were killed and 90 injured in the attack. Bomb damage to the harbour facilities also delayed the refitting of the *Scharnhorst*, leading to the fatal decision by the German Naval Command to send the *Bismarck* on her Atlantic sortie accompanied only by the *Prinz Eugen*.

With the arrival of the latter at Brest following the destruction of the *Bismarck*, conditions in the harbour became dangerously overcrowded, and it was decided to redeploy the *Scharnhorst* to La Pallice, a port to the south of her original location, where her refitting was completed. While undergoing sea trials to prove some new equipment she was detected by air reconnaissance, and a major daylight attack was mounted against both Brest and La Pallice. The plan called for Brest to be attacked by 79 unescorted Vickers Wellington bombers, while diversionary sorties were to be flown by 18 Handley Page Hampdens, escorted by three squadrons of Spitfires fitted with long-range tanks, and by three Boeing Fortress Is, the latter bombing from 9150m (30,000ft). As a further diversionary measure, the Cherbourg docks were to be attacked by 36 Bristol Blenheims, with a strong Spitfire escort. Meanwhile, the *Scharnhorst* at La Pallice was to be attacked by 15 Handley Page Halifax four-engined heavy bombers. The operation was scheduled to take place on 24 July 1941.

The *Scharnhorst* survives

The Brest attack, in the event, was a disaster. The raid was broken up by fierce fighter opposition; 10 Wellingtons and two Hampdens were shot down by fighters or flak, and the warships in the harbour were not hit. The Halifaxes attacking La Pallice also met strong fighter opposition and some flak. The result was that five were shot down and all the others damaged. However, five direct hits were registered on the *Scharnhorst*. Three armour-piercing bombs went straight through the vessel, and between 3048 and 7112 tonnes (3000 and 7000 tons) of water poured into her through the resulting holes. Two smaller bombs exploded in the battery deck, but caused negligible damage and there were no casualties. That night the *Scharnhorst* returned to Brest, making 50km/h (27 knots) despite the volume of water inside her, to take advantage of that port's better repair facilities and stronger flak defences. It would be four months

before she was fully seaworthy again and able to re-enter the war.

At the beginning of 1942, against the depressing backdrop of Allied reverses in the Far East and North Africa, Admiral Sir John Tovey, the Commander-in-Chief, Home Fleet, had two main anxieties. The first concerned the German Brest Squadron – the *Scharnhorst*, *Gneisenau* and *Prinz Eugen* – now believed to be battleworthy again, and the second arose through the movement of the new and very powerful battleship *Tirpitz* to join the Trondheim Squadron in mid-January, clearly to form the nucleus of a powerful battle group for operations against the Allied Arctic and North Atlantic convoys.

On 12 January, following a further attack on the warships at Brest by RAF Bomber Command, Adolf Hitler decided that the vessels must be moved if they were to avoid further damage, and since there was little likelihood that they might break out into the Atlantic unscathed, only two options remained open. The first was to return them to Germany by means of a high-speed dash through the English Channel; the second was to decommission them.

The 'Channel dash'

Faced with such a choice, Vice-Admiral Ciliax, commanding the Brest Squadron, produced an outline plan for a breakout operation, which was allocated the code-name 'Cerberus'. (In Greek mythology, Cerberus was the three-headed dog that guarded the gates of Hell). The ships would leave Brest at night to avoid detection for as long as possible, and they would pass through the Straits of Dover in daylight, placing them in a better position to fight off torpedo attacks by surface vessels and aircraft. Also, they would have full advantage of the strong air umbrella that could be provided by the Luftwaffe.

The British maintained their surveillance of Brest throughout January, and on 25 January air reconnaisance showed that all three ships had left their berths and were in the main harbour. The photographs also showed an increasing number of supporting craft at Brest and concentrations of S-boats at various Channel ports.

On 2 February, the Admiralty distributed to all authorities a study of the various alternatives open to the Germans, in which it was concluded that their most probable course of action was a dash through the Channel to their home bases. The main burden of countering this move would fall not on the Home Fleet, but on the naval commands at Plymouth, Portsmouth and Dover,

especially on the latter, whose forces would be most favourably placed for interception. As a preliminary step the Admiralty ordered certain redeployments of destroyers, submarines, minelayers and MTBs. To supplement these forces, six Swordfish of No 825 Squadron, Fleet Air Arm, were deployed to Manston in Kent on 4 February; every available aircraft of Bomber Command was bombed-up and placed on two hours' readiness, No 19 Group of Coastal Command stepped up its surveillance of the southwestern approaches, and Fighter Command stood ready to provide air cover. After a week, however, the state of readiness was downgraded and squadrons released for other operations, with the proviso that they would immediately be switched to anti-shipping operations if need be.

On 8 February, British Intelligence received a warning from the French Resistance that the warships were making ready to sail, and subsequent air reconnaissance showed the *Scharnhorst* and *Prinz Eugen* in the harbour and the *Gneisenau* just outside. Armed with this knowledge, and with information to the effect that weather

ABOVE The Scharnhorst. *The 28cm (11in) guns were retained in the German battlecruisers to permit a greater proportion of weight to protection. When built, their displacement was announced as 26,417 tonnes (26,000 tons) to conform with treaty restrictions. In fact it was considerably more than this.*

conditions would be favourable for a breakout within 48 hours, the Admiralty and Air Ministry concluded that the Germans would make their attempt during the week beginning 10 February. On the 11th, air reconnaissance revealed that the three warships were once again in the main harbour, with six destroyers and a concentration of smaller craft. RAF Bomber Command carried out a small-scale attack during the night, but its only result was to delay the start of the breakout by an hour.

The ships eventually formed up in the roads outside Brest at 2245 hours, and now began an unfortunate chain of circumstances that was to deprive the British of vital intelligence of their movements. A French Resistance agent saw them sail, but was unable to reach his transmitter because of a strong security cordon around the harbour. A Coastal Command Hudson patrol aircraft had to return early with radar failure, and its replacement detected nothing at all, even though the enemy ships were well within range of its ASV (Air to Surface Vessel) radar. No replacement arrived to cover the gap left by this aircraft, and the fact that this stretch of the coastline was no longer being watched was not reported to the Admiralty. In fact, the third patrol Hudson had been recalled because of fog; had it reached its station, patrolling an area off the Sussex coast, it would almost certainly have detected the group of German warships at first light.

By that time the Brest Squadron was steaming at full-speed off Barfleur, following a channel swept by eight

BELOW *A Handley Page Halifax of RAF Bomber Command on a bombing run over the* Scharnhorst *and* Gneisenau *at Brest. The battlecruisers can be seen top centre, with a smokescreen just beginning to develop. The French Atlantic ports suffered much collateral damage during these air attacks.*

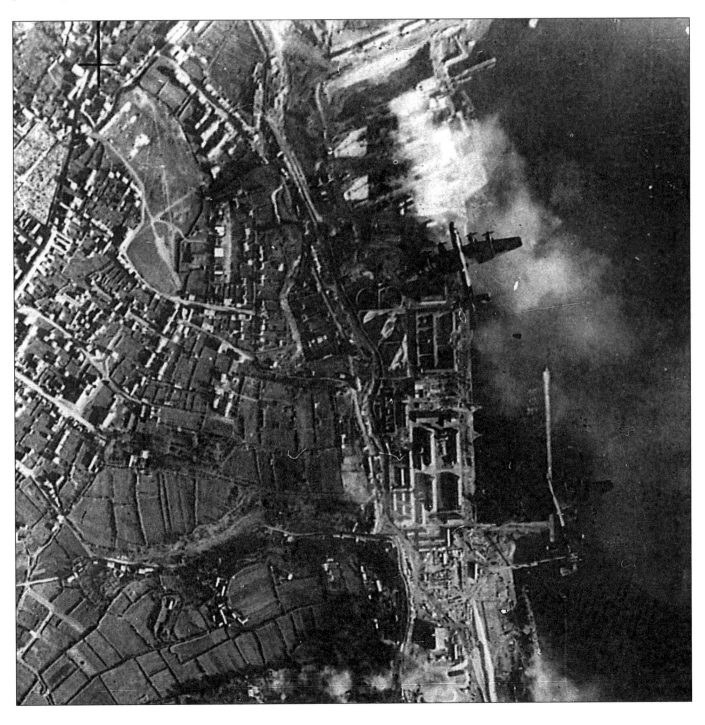

minesweeping flotillas in the preceding weeks and escorted by six destroyers. At the narrowest stretch of the Channel, between Le Havre and Dunkirk, the force would be strengthened by 14 vessels of the 2nd, 3rd and 5th Torpedo-Boat Flotillas, while the 2nd and 6th S-boat Flotillas would join the escort in the North Sea. Air Fleet 3 had allocated 176 bombers and fighters (mainly the Me109s and FW190s of JGs 2 and 26) to the operation, covering the force with relays of at least 16 aircraft at all times.

For almost 13 hours the Brest Squadron sailed on unmolested, even though it had been sighted by the pilots of two sections of patrolling Spitfires, at least one of whom broke radio silence to report the warships' position. The subsequent slowness of the British reaction can only be explained by a communications breakdown somewhere along the line. It must be said, however, that the German ships were greatly helped by the weather conditions, which effectively ruled out air attack at this time. The Royal Navy's surface units were also poorly placed for an attack; the destroyers were exercising in the North Sea, and the small force of MTBs at Ramsgate had suffered in an engagement during the night.

At 1120 hours, the German force reduced speed to 10 knots to allow sweepers to clear a path through the minefield laid by British destroyers. The passage took 20 minutes and the ships once again went ahead at full

ABOVE *Cut-away diagram showing the internal design of the* Scharnhorst. *The design of the* Scharnhorst *and* Gneisenau *was based on that of the Mackensen class battlecruisers which failed to challenge the superiority of the Royal Navy in World War I, and which in turn were improved and enlarged vessels of the Derfflinger type.*

speed; a golden opportunity to attack them during the interval had been lost. At 1218 hours the gun batteries at Dover – the first units to try to engage the enemy – opened fire on the warships, but their shells fell short. At the same time, five MTBs from Dover under Lieutenant-Commander Pumphrey began their attack run, heading for the outer screen of torpedo-boats and the destroyers beyond, the latter laying a smokescreen. The battlecruisers were visible beyond the smoke and Pumphrey signalled their position, speed and course, information that was relayed to the MTBs at Ramsgate and the Fleet Air Arm detachment at Manston. Bereft of any support from fighter-bombers or MGBs, both of which had been promised, Pumphrey's small force tried to slip through the escort screen. Intense fire from the escort vessels and enemy aircraft forced the MTBs to split up and make individual attacks; most of their torpedoes were launched at a range of two miles or more, and no hits were observed.

Meanwhile, alerted by the MTBs' signals, the six Swordfish of No 825 Squadron had taken off from

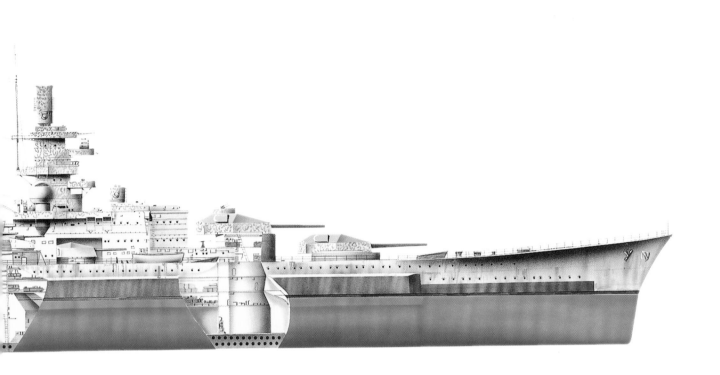

SPECIFICATIONS: *SCHARNHORST*

GENERAL

Ship type: Battlecruiser

Entered service: 1939

Complement: 1800

Fate: Sunk by *Duke of York* 26/12/43

MACHINERY

Engine: Diesel

Power: Three screws, geared turbines

ARMOUR

Belt: 70–350mm (2.7–13.6in)

Deck: 50–105mm (2–4in)

Turrets: 150–360mm (5.8–14in)

ARMAMENT

Main: Nine 280mm (11in), 12 150mm (6in) guns

Secondary: 14 105mm (4in), 16 37mm (1.5in) AA guns; six 53cm (21in) torpedo tubes

DIMENSIONS

Length: 229.8m (754ft)

Width: 30m (98ft 6in)

Height: 9.9m (32ft 6in)

Displacement: 32,514 tonnes (32,000 tons)

PERFORMANCE

Speed: 57km/h (31 knots)

Manston, led by Lieutenant-Commander Eugene Esmonde, at 1225 hours. Esmonde had been promised an escort of five Spitfire squadrons, but a combination of bad weather and a timing error resulted in only 10 Spitfires turning up three minutes after the Swordfish had set course.

Within 10 minutes the Spitfires were engaged in a fierce low-level battle with enemy fighters, in the course of which they lost contact with the Swordfish. The latter, flying in two sections of three, pressed on unescorted towards the warships, harassed by fighters all the way. The pilots of the first three Swordfish selected the

Scharnhorst as they broke through the outer screen and launched their torpedoes. Lieutenant-Commander Esmonde went down into the sea immediately afterwards and the other two Swordfish were forced down within a minute or so, five of their six crew members later being picked up alive by the MTBs.

The second flight of Swordfish was seen passing over the torpedo-boat screen, then the three aircraft vanished in the smoke and the geysers of water flung up by the cruisers' armament. All three were shot down and their crews killed. Of the 18 crew involved in the operation, therefore, only five survived. Lieutenant-Commander

ABOVE *A German lookout on one of the German battlecruisers, muffled against the cold of a February day, gazes at the destroyers and torpedo boats assigned to escort the* Scharnhorst, Gneisenau *and* Prinz Eugen *on their daring dash through the English Channel in February 1942.*

Esmonde, who had not expected to return, was posthumously awarded the Victoria Cross.

It was now 1300 hours and the warships, still unscathed, were passing Ramsgate, from where three MTBs under Lieutenant-Commander Long set out to attack them. Like their colleagues at Dover, they found the enemy's defensive screen too strong to penetrate and they were soon left behind, returning to harbour in rapidly deteriorating weather and rising seas. But trouble for the Brest Squadron was not far over the horizon: at 1421 hours, while passing at reduced speed through another dangerous bottleneck – the Ruytingen Narrows – the *Scharnhorst* struck a mine. Her engines were temporarily stopped and it was half an hour before she could get

under way – half an hour during which not a single British aircraft was sighted. Admiral Ciliax and his staff were transferred to the leading destroyer by cutter, only to be transferred again when the warship was damaged by the premature explosion of one of its own shells.

At about 1445 hours aircraft of Bomber Command arrived overhead, and before nightfall the Command had flown 242 sorties against the ships, although only one in six managed to bomb them. They succeeded in sinking the patrol ship V1302 and in damaging the torpedo boats T13 and *Jaguar*. Attacks by Beaufort torpedo bombers were fragmented and produced no result. In all, the RAF lost 41 aircraft, including 17 fighters; the Luftwaffe's losses amounted to 17 aircraft.

The assault by the first wave of bombers coincided with an attempted attack by six destroyers from Harwich, the *Campbell, Mackay, Vivacious, Worcester, Whitshed* and *Walpole*, led by Captains C.T.M. Pizey and J.P. Wright. The *Walpole* developed mechanical trouble and returned to Harwich, leaving the other five to execute the attack. It was a hazardous operation; not only did the destroyer crews have to contend with enemy fire, but they also had to thread their way through a British minefield – which luckily was clearly marked on their charts – and run the gauntlet of British bombs. The ships reached the outer screen at about 1530 hours and initiated individual attacks on the *Gneisenau* and other vessels, but intense fire from the battlecruisers' heavy armament kept the destroyers at arm's length and they were forced to launch their torpedoes at long range. Only one destroyer, HMS *Worcester*, came within 2700m (3000 yards); she was badly damaged and set on fire, limping back to Harwich with four of her crew dead and 19 wounded and coming close to being attacked by a Beaufort en route. Once again, the German warships were unharmed.

The Brest Squadron slipped away into the darkness. Just before 2000 hours the *Gneisenau* struck a mine, but sustained no very serious injury. Ninety minutes later, however, the *Scharnhorst* was mined a second time and came to a stop, but by that time the British had lost touch with the enemy and were unable to take advantage of this development. On 13 February, the *Scharnhorst* limped to safety in Wilhelmshaven while the other two warships went on to the Elbe Estuary.

A blow for British pride

The 'Channel Dash' had been an undisputed success for the Germans, and for the British a woeful tale of incompetence, bad planning and humiliation for which not even the courage of the Royal Navy and RAF could compensate. Yet for the enemy, the sequel to the operation was not a happy one. The *Gneisenau* was hit by Bomber Command in Kiel harbour a fortnight after Cerberus and never went to sea again; her gun turrets were removed for coastal defence and she was sunk as a blockship at Gdynia, where she was seized by the Russians and broken up between 1947 and 1951.

Only the *Scharnhorst* re-emerged in due course to threaten Allied shipping on the high seas. On 1 April 1942, Captain Hoffmann, who had commanded the battlecruiser for three years and who had now been promoted to Rear-Admiral, handed over command of the ship to Captain Huffmeier. In October that year, the *Scharnhorst* was pronounced battleworthy again, and on 11 January 1943, together with the *Prinz Eugen* and three destroyers, she attempted a move to Norway to join the Trondheim Squadron. West of the Skagerrak, however, the ships were sighted by British reconnaissance aircraft, and, through fear of losing another capital ship,

she was ordered to return to the relative safety of a German port.

A second transfer attempt, in stormy weather on 8 March 1943 (without the *Prinz Eugen*) was successful, and on 11 March, the *Scharnhorst* and *Tirpitz*, accompanied by destroyers and torpedo boats, moved up from Trondheim to Bogen Bay near Narvik to join the heavy cruiser *Lützow*, which was already there. On 22 March the heavy units moved again, this time to Altenfjord.

On 6 September 1943, the *Scharnhorst* accompanied the *Tirpitz* on Operation 'Sicily', the landing of troops and bombardment of shore stations on Spitzbergen, described earlier. She did not put to sea again until December, and this time it was to engage the Arctic convoys. After an interval of several months, when no convoys had passed to the Soviet Union because of the dangers involved, they had resumed in November when Convoy RA54A sailed from Archangel to the UK without incident; two more outward-bound convoys, JW54A and JW54B, also made the journey from Loch Ewe to Russia unmolested. The next two convoys, however, were both reported by the Luftwaffe, and Admiral Dönitz issued orders that they were to be attacked not only by the 24 U-boats based on Bergen and Trondheim, but by available surface units, the largest of which was the *Scharnhorst*.

The convoys were JW55B, outward bound from Loch Ewe with 19 ships, and RA55A, homeward bound from Kola. The former sailed on 20 December 1943, the latter three days later. Each was escorted by ten destroyers and a number of smaller vessels.

A fatal decision

At 1400 hours on Christmas Day, the *Scharnhorst* – now under the command of Captain F. Hintze and flying the flag of Admiral Bey, a former commodore of destroyers who had recently been appointed to command the Northern Battle Group – sailed from Norway accompanied by five destroyers to intercept JW55B, which had been located by air reconnaissance on 22 December. The convoy had already been attacked by Ju 88s and by U-boats, but without success. On 26 December, Admiral Bey ordered his destroyers to form a patrol line to search for the convoy in heavy seas. He knew that a British cruiser covering force comprising the *Belfast*, *Norfolk* and *Sheffield* was operating in the Barents Sea; what he did not know was that there was also a distant covering force commanded by the C-in-C Home Fleet, Admiral Sir Bruce Fraser, and comprising the battleship *Duke of York*, the cruiser *Jamaica* and four destroyers, which had sailed from Iceland.

Fraser, aware that JW55B had been located by enemy aircraft, was convinced that the *Scharnhorst* would make a sortie against it, and detached four detroyers from Convoy RA55A, which he did not consider to be under immediate threat, to reinforce JW55B's close escort. His hope was that this strengthened destroyer force would not only be sufficient to drive off the *Scharnhorst*, but might perhaps damage her enough for the *Duke of York* to come up and finish her off. At this point Admiral Fraser's ships were 370km (200nm) SW of North Cape and the cruiser force, under Admiral Burnett, 278km (150nm) to the east.

Admiral Bey's five destroyers, meanwhile, had not only failed to locate the convoy; they had also, because of a signalling error, lost touch with the flagship and were subsequently ordered to return to base, so that they took no part in the coming events.

The battle begins

At 0840 hours on 26 December, the cruisers *Norfolk* and *Belfast* obtained radar contact with the *Scharnhorst* at 35,000 yards, and at 0921 hours, the *Sheffield* glimpsed her in the stormy darkness at 11,895m (13,000 yards). A few minutes later all three destroyers opened fire on the battlecruiser and obtained three hits, one of which put her port 15cm (6in) fire control system out of action. The *Scharnhorst* replied with a few harmless 28cm (11in) salvoes, then Bey turned away to the southeast while Burnett placed his cruisers between the threat and the convoy, screened by four destroyers from the escort.

At 1221 hours the three cruisers again sighted the *Scharnhorst* and opened fire with full broadsides at 10,065m (11,000 yards), while the destroyers fanned out to attack with torpedoes. Before they were able to get into position the battlecruiser retired to the northeast, her gunfire having put one of *Norfolk*'s turrets and all her radar out of action; *Sheffield* also suffered some splinter damage. But the *Scharnhorst* had taken some punishment too, including a hit abreast 'A' turret and one on her quarterdeck.

At 1617 hours, the *Duke of York*, now 37km (20nm) away to the northeast, obtained a radar echo from the *Scharnhorst*. At 1650 hours Fraser ordered *Belfast* to illuminate her with starshell, and immediately afterwards the *Duke of York* opened fire with her 35.5cm (14in) armament. Admiral Bey was now trapped between Burnett's cruisers to the north and Fraser's warships to the south,

and he had no choice but to fight it out. Once *Scharnhorst*'s gunners had recovered from their surprise their fire was accurate, but although they straddled the British battleship many times they failed to register a serious hit on her. The *Duke of York*'s gunnery was excellent; she scored 31 straddles out of 52 broadsides, with enough hits to put the battlescruiser's 'A' and 'B' turrets out of action and to rupture some steam pipes, which reduced her speed so that Admiral Bey had no chance of outrunning his adversaries, even if the opportunity had arisen.

The end of the *Scharnhorst*

At 1824 hours, the third of *Scharnhorst*'s turrets was put out of action, and Fraser, realising that the *Duke of York*'s 35.5cm (14in) shells, fired at short range with a flat trajectory, were unlikely to pierce the enemy's armour, turned away to let the destroyers finish the job. Two of them, the *Savage* and *Saumarez*, approached from the northwest under heavy fire, firing starshell, while *Scorpion* and *Stord* attacked fom the southeast, launching their torpedoes at 1849 hours. As Hintze turned his ship to port to engage them, one of *Scorpion*'s torpedoes struck home, closely followed by three more from the first two destroyers. As the small ships retired under cover of smoke, the *Duke of York* and the cruisers closed in to batter the enemy warship with merciless fire. As Lieutenant B.B. Ramsden, an officer of Royal Marines on HMS *Jamaica*, later wrote that the *Scharnhorst* 'must have been a hell on earth. The 14-inch from the flagship were hitting or rocketing off from a ricochet on the sea. Great flashes rent the night, and the sound of gunfire was continuous, and yet she replied, but only occasionally now with what armament she had left.'

By 1930 hours, the battlecruiser was a blazing wreck, and the destroyers closed in to finish her off with torpedoes. At 1945 hours she blew up, and only 36 of her crew of 1,968 officers and men were rescued from the freezing seas. So ended what would come to be known as the the Battle of North Cape, and with it the last significant attempt by a capital ship of the German Navy to challenge the supremacy of the Royal Navy.

RIGHT *Blindfolded survivors of the* Scharnhorst, *in merchant seamen's rescue kit, being taken ashore at a British port on their way to a British prisoner-of-war camp. The German naval personnel later recorded that the British sailors who had rescued them treated them with great kindness.*

CHAPTER 4

THE HEAVY AND LIGHT CRUISER FORCES

Of all the German surface forces to see action in World War II, operations by the cruiser forces – particularly the heavy cruisers – were perhaps handled most intelligently. While the German Admiralty was not prepared to risk its battleships against superior odds, its cruisers sometimes engaged far greater forces, especially in the Arctic battles against the convoys.

O f the five heavy cruisers at Germany's disposal in 1939, one, the *Lützow*, was sold to the USSR early in 1940. Another, the *Seydlitz*, did not see action, being scuttled at Königsberg on 10 April 1945.

In February 1940 the former 'pocket battleships' *Deutschland*, now renamed *Lützow* after the transfer of

LEFT *The British destroyer* Glowworm, *while off the Norwegian coast, encountered German forces, heading for Trondheim on 8 April 1940. After ramming the* Admiral Hipper, *she was sunk by gunfire from the German cruiser, whose bow is visible in this photograph.*

the original ship bearing that name to the Soviet Union, and the *Admiral Scheer* were both reclassified heavy cruisers, so that by the time of the German invasion of Norway, the Navy's heavy cruiser force comprised these two ships, the *Admiral Hipper* and the *Blücher*, with the *Prinz Eugen* fitting out. In July 1940, the latter was slightly damaged by two small bombs during an RAF raid on Kiel; her fortunes as *Bismarck*'s consort and in the months following the sinking of the battleship we have already seen.

On 21 February 1942, 10 days after the 'Channel Dash,' she sailed for Norway in company with the *Admiral Scheer* and four destroyers; the German force

was located by British reconnaissance aircraft in the North Sea and subjected to bombing attacks, one bomber being shot down by the *Prinz Eugen*'s anti-aircraft guns. On the following day the warships were again located by reconnaissance aircraft, and on 23 February she was attacked off Trondheim by the submarine HMS *Trident* (Commander Sladen), receiving a heavy torpedo hit in the stern. Still under Captain Brinkmann's command, she put into Trondheim for emergency repairs, leaving on 16 May with an escort of destroyers and torpedo boats. The next day, en route for Germany, she was attacked by 12 Beaufort torpedo-bombers and six Blenheims; the attack was unsuccessful, three aircraft being lost to anti-aircraft fire and Me109s. Four more aircraft were shot down by fighters during subsequent attacks. The warship arrived in Kiel on 18 May.

Aiding the ground war

In 1943, after her abortive attempt to break through to Norway in January, she was assigned to the Baltic Training Squadron, and in August 1944 she was used as a fire support ship against a concentration of Soviet troops who had broken through near Tukkum on the Gulf of Riga. With the help of her gunfire, and that of destroyers, the

ABOVE *The 'pocket battleship'* Admiral Scheer *seen before the war. When she was reclassified as a heavy cruiser, she received a new raked bow; a new control tower and foremast replaced the original armoured tower, which can be seen in this photograph, and her anti-aircraft armament was increased.*

Germans were able to restore communications with Army Group North, temporarily cut off by the Soviet attack. In October, now commanded by Captain Reinicke, she was again in action against Soviet forces who had broken through to the Baltic between Libau and Memel, and in November she covered shipping evacuating troops and civilians from the Sworbe peninsula, under heavy attack by the Soviet 8th Army.

She saw heavy action late on in the war. In January and February 1945, during the Soviet assault on East Prussia, she was enlisted to stem the tide of the Soviet advance and – as flagship of Vice-Admiral Thiele's Task Force 2 – shelled forward Soviet armour from the Königsberg Sea Canal. In March she joined with other warships in covering the evacuation of refugees from the Danzig area, menaced by an assault by the Soviet 2nd White Russian Front.

In the final days of the war she sailed for Copenhagen, where her crew surrendered to British naval forces on 9 May 1945. Late in May she was taken under escort to Wilhelmshaven. She was subsequently allocated to the USA as war booty. She participated as a target ship in the atomic bomb trials at Bikini Atoll in June 1946, in which a Nagasaki-type bomb was dropped on 73 vessels, and having survived that experience – in which five ships were sunk and nine damaged – she was finally sunk at Kwajalein in 1947.

The *Blücher*

One early heavy cruiser casualty of the war was the *Blücher*. During the invasion of Norway on 9 April 1940, she was the flagship of Group Five of the invasion force, flying the flag of Rear-Admiral Kummetz; the naval force, carrying 2000 troops, was bound for Oslo, the Norwegian capital. Proceeding at only 22km/h (12 knots) through

BELOW *The heavy cruiser* Blücher *had a short career. Launched in June 1937, she is seen here ablaze and sinking after being torpedoed in Oslofjord during the German invasion of Norway on 9 April 1940. More than 50 years later, she was starting to become a pollution hazard as oil leaked from her corroded tanks.*

the Drobak Narrows – the entrance to Oslofjord, only 500 yards wide at that point – she was hit at point-blank range by the 20cm (8in) and 28cm (11in) guns of the defending forts and set ablaze; torpedoes from the forts did the rest, reducing her to a helpless hulk. At 0630 hours she capsized and sank with the loss of over 1000 officers and men. Her wreck was still there in the 1990s, an increasing pollution hazard as oil seeped from corroded tanks.

The *Admiral Hipper*

The last of the five original German heavy cruisers launched before World War II, the *Admiral Hipper* made her first war sortie on 18 February 1940, when she accompanied the *Scharnhorst* and *Gneisenau* on Operation 'Nordmark', the search for Allied convoys between Britain and Scandinavia. During the invasion of Norway she was the flagship of Task Group 2, whose objective was Trondheim. As the German task groups headed for their objectives, the British minelaying destroyers *Esk*, *Icarus*, *Impulsive* and *Ivanhoe*, escorted by the destroyers *Hardy*, *Havock*, *Hotspur* and *Hunter*, were laying a mine barrage off Bodö on 8 April. The covering force comprised the battlecruiser *Renown* and the destroyers *Hyperion*, *Hero*, *Greyhound* and

Glowworm, and it was the latter that made the first contact with the German ships. Detached to make a vain search for a seaman swept overboard from *Renown* during a storm on 8 April, she sighted the warships of Task Group Two, bound for Trondheim. *Glowworm* fired two salvoes at an enemy destroyer before the latter was lost to sight in heavy seas and fog; a few minutes later a second destroyer came into view and *Glowworm* gave chase, the two warships exchanging shot for shot. The larger German vessel increased speed in an attempt to shake off her adversary but her bow ploughed under, forcing her to slow down. *Glowworm* closed in, her captain, Lieutenant-Commander G.B. Roope, trying to get into position for a shot with torpedoes.

Some distance ahead, a great, dark shape burst from a fog bank. For a few seconds the men on *Glowworm*'s bridge were elated, believing the ship to be HMS *Renown*. Then a salvo of heavy shells struck the British destroyer, setting her on fire. The newcomer was the *Admiral Hipper*.

The sacrifice of the *Glowworm*

Roope sheered off for long enough to radio a report, then turned back towards the German cruiser in the hope of torpedoing her. When this proved impossible he headed his burning ship straight for the *Hipper*, ramming her

ABOVE *Cut-away diagram of the* Admiral Hipper *as she appeared after modification in 1939–40, with new bow, funnel and tower. The other vessels in the Hipper class were the* Lützow (sold to the USSR), Seydlitz, Blücher *and* Prinz Eugen. *Work began on converting the* Seydlitz *as an aircraft carrier, but it was never completed.*

starboard bow, tearing off 40m (130ft) of her armour belt and wrenching away her starboard torpedo tubes. The cruiser's captain, H. Heye, ordered his guns to hold their fire as the *Glowworm* fell away, ablaze and doomed. A few minutes later, at 0900 hours, she blew up.

Captain Heye ordered his ship's crew to search for surivors. They plucked 38 from the sea. Lieutenant-Commander Roope himself reached the cruiser's side, but was too exhausted to hold on to the rope German sailors threw to him, and was drowned. His matchless courage earned him a posthumous Victoria Cross, the first to be won by the Royal Navy in World War II. On 10 April, the damaged *Hipper* left Trondheim and headed south for Germany, accompanied by a destroyer. She was at sea again in June, taking part in the sortie in which the *Scharnhorst* and *Gneisenau* sank the aircraft carrier *Glorious*. During the summer months of 1940 she made several sorties into the Arctic, intent on mercantile warfare, but had no success. Her first attempt to break

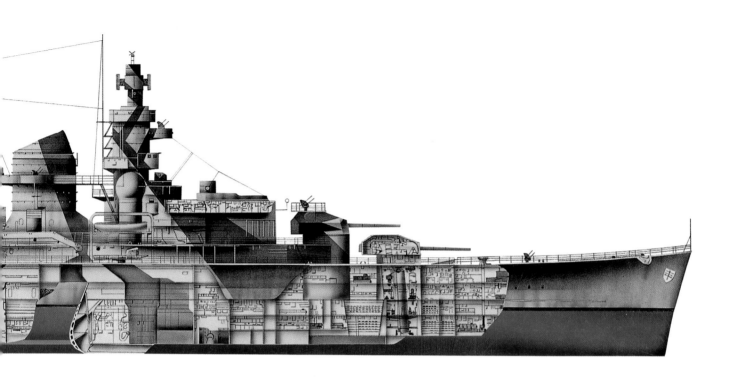

SPECIFICATIONS: *ADMIRAL HIPPER*

GENERAL
Ship type: Heavy cruiser
Entered service: 1939
Complement: 1600
Fate: Bombed then scuttled 4/5/45

MACHINERY
Engine: Diesel
Power: Three-shaft geared turbines

ARMOUR
Belt: 127mm (5in)
Deck: 100mm (4in)
Turrets: 127mm (5in)

ARMAMENT
Eight 20cm (8in), 12 10cm (4in) guns;
12 37mm (1.5in), 8 20mm (0.78in) AA
guns; 12 53cm (21in) torpedo tubes

DIMENSIONS
Length: 195m (640ft)
Width: 21m (70ft)
Height: 4.5m (15ft)
Displacement: 14,123 tonnes
(13,900 tons)

PERFORMANCE
Speed: 59km/h (32 knots)

out into the Atlantic on mercantile warfare operations, on 24 September, ended in failure when she developed serious engine trouble west of Stavanger and had to return to Kiel; on the second attempt, commanded by Captain Meisel, she succeeded, passing unobserved through the Denmark Strait.

Hunting the convoys

On 24 December, 1297km (700nm) to the west of Cape Finisterre, on the northwest tip of Spain, she intercepted the British troop convoy WS5A, comprising 20 ships bound for the Mediterranean. The convoy was escorted by the cruisers *Berwick*, *Bonaventure* and *Dunedin* and accompanied by the carriers *Argus* and *Furious*, destined for Takoradi on the west coast of Africa with reinforcement aircraft for the Middle East. Captain Meisel decided to attack, and in the ensuing engagement, on 25 December, the *Hipper*'s gunners hit the *Berwick* twice and damaged two transports. Because of engine trouble, which might have left his ship at the mercy of the British warships, Meisel elected to break off the attack and head for Brest, sinking one small freighter as he withdrew.

The *Hipper* left Brest on 1 February 1941 for another Atlantic sortie. On 11 February, she located a straggler from a dispersed convoy and sank her, and on 12 February she made contact with nine unescorted ships

of Convoy SLS64, sinking seven of them totalling 33,333 tonnes (32,806 tons) and severely damaging two more. She returned to Brest on 15 February. A month later she sailed for Kiel, arriving on 28 March after an undetected passage through the Denmark Strait. She remained in German waters until 19 March 1942, when she sailed with three destroyers and three torpedo boats to join the Trondheim Squadron.

On 2 July she sailed with the *Tirpitz*, four destroyers and two torpedo boats to attack Convoy PQ17, but the force put into Altenfjord and made no attempt to intercept. The *Hipper* did not make another sortie until 24 September, when, accompanied by a destroyer screen, she carried out a minelaying operation off the northwest coast of Novaya Zemlya. She was at sea again early in November of that year, with a new commander, Captain H. Hartmann. This time she was searching for freighters bound independently for the Soviet Union; she failed to make contact, but her escorting destroyers had some modest success, sinking a Soviet tanker and a submarine-chaser.

ABOVE *The* Admiral Hipper *attacking a ship of Convoy SLS64 on 12 February 1941. The convoy consisted of nine unescorted ships and the* Hipper *sank seven of them before returning to Brest to replenish. Nine ships of another convoy, HG53, were sunk at the same time by U-boats and aircraft.*

On 30 December, Vice-Admiral Oskar Kummetz, commanding the Northern Battle Group, took the *Admiral Hipper* (Captain H. Hartmann), the *Lützow* (Captain R. Stange) and six destroyers out of Altenfjord to attack Convoy JW51B. The convoy, consisting of 14 ships with an escort of six destroyers and five small anti-submarine vessels, had already been sighted on 24 December by the U354 (Lieutenant-Commander Herbschleb), and the German Admiralty had at once initiated Operation 'Regenbogen' ('Rainbow').

Kummetz's tactical options were limited. He was under orders not to risk a night engagement against escorts which might make torpedo attacks on his ships; he was only to engage a force weaker than his own by day; and futhermore the *Lützow* was afterwards to make a sortie into the Atlantic, which meant that she would need to conserve fuel and ammunition, not to mention to avoid damage.

At 0830 hours on 31 December the *Hipper* and her destroyers passed 27km (20nm) astern of the convoy, while the *Lützow* and her escorts were 93km (50nm) to the south and closing. The British cruisers *Sheffield* (Captain A.W. Clarke, flying the flag of Rear-Admiral R.L. Burnett) and *Jamaica* (Captain J.L. Storey) were about 60km (30nm) to the north. The approaching enemy force was sighted by the corvette *Hyderabad*, which, mistaking the German destroyers for expected Soviet escorts, made no report. Ten minutes later the German vessels were also detected by the destroyer *Obdurate*, whose captain, Lieutenant-Commander C.E. Sclater, reported them to the escort commander Lieutenant-Commander R. St V. Sherbrooke, in the flotilla leader HMS

BELOW *The heavy cruiser* Prinz Eugen *firing a salvo. In April 1941, the* Prinz Eugen *was damaged by a magnetic mine; a month later she sailed with the* Bismarck, *taking refuge in Brest after the battleship was sunk. Together with the* Scharnhorst *and* Gneisenau, *she took part in the famous 'Channel Dash' of February 1942.*

Onslow, but did not identify them. Sherbrooke ordered Sclater to investigate and *Obdurate* closed to within 7km (4nm) of the enemy ships, turning away when they opened fire.

Desperate defence

Leaving the destroyer *Achates* and three smaller escorts to protect the convoy with a smokescreen, Sherbrooke headed to join *Obdurate* at full speed, accompanied by the *Obedient* and *Orwell* and transmitting an enemy sighting report to Rear-Admiral Burnett. At 0941 hours the *Hipper* opened fire on the *Achates* and was at once engaged by the *Onslow* and *Orwell*, Sherbrooke sending the other two destroyers to assist in protecting the convoy. At 1020 hours, the *Hipper* found *Onslow*'s range and set her on fire, putting half her armament out of action and holing her engine room. Sherbrooke, badly wounded, was obliged to turn over command to Lieutenant-Commander D.C. Kinloch in the *Obedient*, refusing to leave the bridge until assured that his orders had been received. At the same time, the *Hipper* disappeared into a snow squall. Some minutes later, at 1045 hours, she encountered the little minesweeper *Bramble*, which was armed with only one 10cm (4in) gun, and quickly destroyed her with the loss of her captain, Commander

SPECIFICATIONS: *PRINZ EUGEN*

GENERAL

Ship type: Heavy cruiser

Entered service: 1940

Complement: 1450

Fate: Sunk after Bikini Atoll trials

MACHINERY

Engine: Diesel

Power: Three-shaft geared turbines

ARMOUR

Belt: 127mm (5in)

Deck: 100mm (4in)

Turrets: 127mm (5in)

ARMAMENT

Eight 20cm (8in), 12 10cm (4in) guns; 12 37mm (1.5in), 8 20mm (0.78in) AA guns; 12 53cm (21in) torpedo tubes

DIMENSIONS

Length: 195m (640ft)

Width: 21m (70ft)

Height: 4.5m (15ft)

Displacement: 14,123 tonnes (13,900 tons)

PERFORMANCE

Speed: 59km/h (32 knots)

H.T. Rust, and all his crew. It was a typically heroic engagement by a completely out-classed Royal Navy ship.

A brief respite

As soon as the *Hipper* disappeared Lieutenant-Commander Kinloch instructed all the destroyers to rejoin the convoy, which was now threatened by the *Lützow*, only 3.7km (2nm) away. Stange, however, decided to stand off while the weather cleared, so allowing a golden opportunity to wipe out the merchantmen to slip through his fingers. At 1100 hours, while Kinloch manoeuvred his destroyers between the convoy and the *Lützow* group, the *Hipper* suddenly reappeared to the north and opened fire on the *Achates*, inflicting many casualties and killing her captain, Lieutenant-Commander Johns; she sank early in the afternoon. The *Hipper* then turned her fire on the *Obedient*; the destroyer suffered only light damage but her radio

was put out of action, so that Kinloch was compelled to turn over command to the *Obdurate*'s captain.

The *Hipper* under fire

At 1130 hours, as Hartmann drew away to avoid the destroyers' torpedo attacks, the *Hipper* was suddenly straddled by 24 15cm (6in) shells from the *Sheffield* and *Jamaica*, closing from the north. Burnett had been able to follow the action by means of *Sheffield*'s radar, but the radar picture was confused and it was not until he obtained a positive sighting that Burnett felt able to engage the German cruiser. Three shells hit the *Hipper*, reducing her speed to 52km/h (28 knots), and faced with this new threat Kummetz ordered Hartmann and the destroyer captains to retire to the west.

As they did so, the *Sheffield*'s guns turned on the destroyer *Friedrich Eckoldt* and, in a sober lesson in naval gunnery, quickly reduced her to a blazing wreck, in the evacuation of German troops from East Prussia early in 1945, and on the night of 9–10 April she was badly damaged in an attack on Kiel by RAF bombers. She was scuttled on 3 May of that year and broken up in 1948–9.

The *Lützow*

The other heavy cruiser that fought in the Battle of the Barents Sea, the *Lützow* (ex-'pocket battleship' *Deutschland*), began her war under her new title on 21 November 1939, with a brief armed reconnaissance sortie against merchant shipping in the Skagerrak.

During the invasion of Norway she was part of the force covering Task Group 5, bound for Oslo, being damaged by three hits from shore batteries, and on 8 April she had a narrow escape when the British submarine *Trident* missed her with 10 torpedoes off Skagen.

Early on 11 April, however, the submarine HMS *Spearfish* (Lieutenant J.G. Forbes) was on the surface recharging her batteries after running the gauntlet of enemy warships when the *Lützow* was sighted, returning to Germany at high speed. Forbes fired a salvo of torpedoes at her and one struck her right aft, wrecking her propellers and rudder and leaving her helpless. Unaware that the warship had no anti-submarine escort, and with his batteries still not replenished, Forbes broke off the attack leaving the *Lützow* wallowing in the water. She summoned help and was towed to Kiel in a desperate condition, and it was to be a year before she was ready for sea again – a year in which she might otherwise have been free to prey on Britain's convoys. Given her previous record, the damage done in that year might have been incalculable. As it was, the convoys had a breathing space to keep Britain away from starvation.

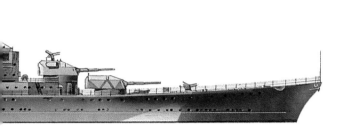

ABOVE *The* Prinz Eugen*'s war continued in the Baltic, where she was deployed to support the German Army against the Russians in 1944. In October that year, however, she was badly damaged in an accidental collision with the light cruiser* Leipzig, *effectively putting her out of action for the duration of the war.*

but the other destroyer, the *Richard Beitzen*, followed the *Hipper* into a snow squall and got away.

The end of the battle

At about 1145 hours, the *Lützow* also opened fire on the convoy from a range of 16,470m (18,000 yards), then she too withdrew as the British destroyers began an attack. There was a further brief engagement between Burnett's cruisers and the enemy force at 1230 hours, in which neither side suffered damage; the Germans continued to retire to the west and contact was lost at 1400 hours.

Three days later, JW51B reached the Kola Inlet without further harm. That was due in no small measure to the tactical skill, leadership and courage of Captain Sherbrooke, who survived to receive the Victoria Cross.

This action, the Battle of the Barents Sea, marked the *Admiral Hipper*'s last sortie in Arctic waters. Transferred to the Fleet Training Squadron in the Baltic, she took part

RIGHT *The* Prinz Eugen *under attack by the* Prince of Wales *during the battle in the Denmark Strait, May 1941, as the cruiser accompanied the* Bismarck. *This picture and other photographs were transferred from the battleship to the cruiser before the two parted company.*

On the night of 8–9 July 1940, while undergoing repairs at Kiel, she escaped further damage when a bomb dropped during an RAF raid hit her and failed to explode, a not uncommon occurrence at this stage of the war. By the summer of 1941, she was battleworthy once more, and on 12 June, under the command of Captain Kreisch, she attempted to break out into the North Atlantic, escorted by five destroyers, to attack merchant shipping. She was sighted by an RAF reconnaissance aircraft off Lindesnes shortly before midnight, and 14 Beaufort torpedo-bombers of Nos 22 and 42 Squadrons were despatched to search for her. She was located by Flight Sergeant R.H. Loveitt of No 42 Squadron, who immediately attacked and secured a torpedo hit amidships. The *Lützow* struggled back to Kiel with partially disabled engines and a heavy list, reaching harbour in the afternoon of 14 June. She was to remain in dock for six months, and Loveitt was awarded a well-deserved Distinguished Flying Medal.

ABOVE *The light cruiser* Königsberg*'s guns in action during a training exercise in 1930.* Königsberg *was the flagship of the senior officer of the German Navy's scouting forces, Vice-Admiral Densch, and was sunk in a dive-bombing attack by Blackburn Skuas of the Fleet Air Arm at Bergen on 10 April 1940.*

It was the last attempt by a surface raider to interfere with the Atlantic convoys; their focus of operations, dictated by the German invasion of the Soviet Union, switched to the Arctic, and it was for that theatre that the *Lützow* sailed in May 1942, arriving at Narvik via Trondheim on the 25th.

The Atlantic threat diminishes

On 3 July 1942, she sailed for Altenfjord to join other surface forces poised for an attack on Soviet convoys, but ran aground in poor visibility. Returning to Germany for repairs, she came back to Norway in December, and this time reached Altenfjord without incident. After her action in the Battle of the Barents Sea, already described, she remained in the Arctic until September 1943, seeing no further action, and then sailed for Gdynia to undergo a refit.

From 29 September 1944, she was on hand to provide fire support for German ground forces fighting the advancing Soviet forces in the Baltic States, joining the *Prinz Eugen* in shelling Russian troop concentrations in the Memel area and covering the evacuation of German personnel from the region. In January–February 1945, now commanded by Captain Knoke, her gunfire supported the German 4th Army, in action against the Soviet 3rd and 48th Armies near Frauenburg in East Prussia, and in March and April she covered the evacuation by sea of German troops and civilians from that area.

BELOW *The* Emden *was the first new cruiser built for the German Navy after World War I. She was intended for overseas service and consequently had large fuel tankage, giving her an endurance of 10,460km (5650nm). Originally a coal-fired vessel, she converted to oil in 1934.*

Afterwards she withdrew to Swinemünde, and it was there, on 16 April 1945, that 18 Lancasters of No 617 Squadron RAF attacked her with Tallboy bombs. A near miss by one bomb tore a large hole in her bottom and she sank in shallow water at her moorings after being driven aground. On 4 May she was blown up and scuttled to prevent her capture by Soviet forces. In September 1947 the wreck was refloated and towed to Leningrad, where it was broken up in the following year.

The *Admiral Scheer*

The *Lützow*'s sister ship, the *Admiral Scheer*, was the most successful of all the German heavy cruisers. After spending most of 1940 refitting at Gdynia, she sailed on her mercantile warfare mission on 23 October, under the command of Captain Krancke, passing undetected through the Denmark Strait on 1 November after a replenishment stop at Stavanger. On 5 November, after sinking a solitary freighter, she attacked Convoy HX84, homeward bound from Halifax with 37 merchantmen and escorted only by the Armed Merchant Cruiser *Jervis Bay*. The latter's captain, E.S.F. Fegen, at once ordered the convoy to scatter under cover of a smokescreen and engaged the Scheer. The *Jervis Bay* was sunk with the

---

SPECIFICATIONS: *EMDEN*

GENERAL

Ship type: Light cruiser

Entered service: 1926

Complement: 630

Fate: Scuttled at Kiel, May 1945

MACHINERY

Engine: Diesel

Power: Twin screw, turbines

ARMOUR

Belt: 76–100mm (3–4in)

Turrets: 51mm (2in)

ARMAMENT

Eight 15cm (6in) guns

DIMENSIONS

Length: 155m (509ft)

Width: 14m (47ft)

Height: 6.6m (21ft 8in)

Displacement: 7102 tonnes (6990 tons)

PERFORMANCE

Speed: 54km/h (29 knots)

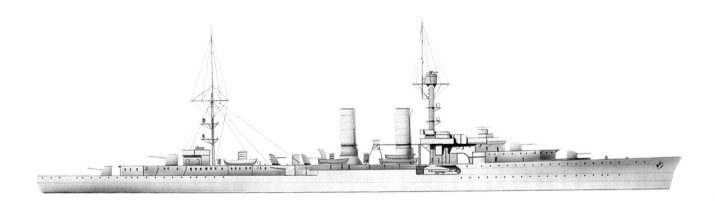

loss of 191 crew, but Fegen's action (which earned him a posthumous Victoria Cross) had bought vital time for the convoy, which lost five ships to the *Scheer*'s guns. She also damaged three more, one of which was the tanker *San Demetrio*. Sixteen men of her crew, who had abandoned the burning vessel, sighted her again 20 hours later and brought their lifeboat alongside; they boarded her, extinguished the fires after a struggle lasting two days, and brought her to harbour in Northern Ireland. Their exploit was made into a propaganda film. (There was, however, a sad end to the *San Demetrio* story. On 17 March 1942, she was torpedoed by U404 east of Chesapeake Bay, and this time she did not survive.)

Upon receipt of the *Jervis Bay*'s distress call the Admiralty deployed naval forces to block the Iceland–Faeroes passage and the approaches to Brest, but by that time the *Scheer* was on her way to the South Atlantic, where, on 18 December, she captured the British refrigeration ship *Duquesa*. The aircraft carriers Formidable and Hermes, together with four cruisers, embarked on a search for the raider, but without result.

A heavy toll

On 18–19 January 1941, the *Scheer* captured three British merchantmen and sailed into the Indian Ocean, where on 14 February she made rendezvous with the commerce raider Schiff 16 *Atlantis* and the supply ship *Tannenfels* 1850km (1000nm) east of Madagascar.

On 20 February her spotter aircraft located two merchant vessels off the Seychelles; the cruiser closed in, capturing the 7106-tonne (6994-ton) *British Advocate* and sinking the smaller Greek *Grigorios CII*. A third ship, the Canadian *Cruiser*, was sunk on the following day, and a Dutch steamer on 22 February. Again, British naval forces, alerted by distress calls, searched in vain for the *Scheer*, which returned to the South Atlantic on 3 March.

On 26–27 March she evaded a British warship screen, passed through the Denmark Strait, and after a stop in Grimstadfjord (Bergen) she arrived in Kiel on 1 April 1941. During her sortie, she had sunk 17 ships totalling 115,050 tonnes (113,233 tons).

On 4 September 1941 the *Scheer* made a brief deployment to Oslo, where Fortress I bombers of the RAF made an unsuccessful high-level attack on her. The four aircraft involved were intercepted by German fighters before they reached the target area; two were shot down and a third crashed in England. The cruiser returned to Germany on 8 September, and on 23 September she joined the *Tirpitz* and other heavy units in blockading an anticipated breakout into the Baltic by the Soviet fleet.

Hunting the Arctic convoys

In February 1942, together with the *Prinz Eugen* – which was torpedoed en route – and five destroyers, she sailed for Norway, and in May she was transferred from Trondheim to Narvik for operations against the Allied convoys to the Soviet Union. Although she was at sea during the operations against Convoy PQ17 in July, she was not actively engaged; but on 16 August, now under the command of Captain Meendsen-Bohlken, she sailed to attack Soviet shipping in the Kara Sea, off northern Siberia between Novaya Zemlya and Severnaya Zemlya. On 25 August she sank the Soviet icebreaker *Sibiryakov* (Captain Kacharev), which put up a valiant defence, and on 27 August she bombarded the naval base at Dikson, severely damaging shore installations, a patrol ship and a steamer.

She returned to Narvik on 30 August. The Kara Sea action was the *Admiral Scheer*'s last offensive sortie in Arctic waters. She was subsequently assigned to the Fleet Training Squadron in the Baltic, taking part in the evacuation of the Sworbe Peninsula in November 1944 under the command of Captain Thienemann and providing fire support for German forces in East Prussia in February 1945. Her last action, in March 1945, was to cover the German forces defending the Wollin bridgehead in Eastern Pomerania. On the night of 9–10 April 1945 she was hit and capsized during a heavy attack on Kiel by RAF Bomber Command; her wreck was later buried under rubble when the basin in which she lay was filled in after the war.

Light cruisers

Of the six light cruisers available to the German Navy at the outbreak of World War II, two were sunk during the Norwegian campaign. During the invasion, the *Karlsrühe* (Captain Rieve) was the flagship of Task Group 4, heading for Kristiansand; on 9 April she was torpedoed by the British submarine *Truant* (Lieutenant-Commander Hutchinson) and was so badly damaged that she had to be sunk later by a German torpedo boat. The next day the *Königsberg* (Captain Ruhfus), part of the Bergen-bound Task Group 3, fell victim to an air attack.

Early in the morning of 10 April 1940, 16 Blackburn Skua dive-bombers of the Fleet Air Arm – seven of No 800 Squadron led by Lieutenant W.P. Lucy, RN and nine of No 803 led by Captain R.T. Partridge, Royal Marines – took

off from Hatston, north of Kirkwall in the Orkneys, each aircraft carrying a 226kg (500lb) bomb. Their target was the German naval force at Bergen, which included the light cruisers *Königsberg* and *Köln* and the gunnery training ship *Bremse*. The ships had already been attacked by Hampdens of RAF Bomber Command during the night, but without success.

After a gruelling 300-mile flight in darkness, the Skuas – their number reduced to 15 after one aircraft returned with engine trouble – made landfall on the Norwegian coast just as the sun was coming up and climbed to 2440m (8000ft), making their dive-bombing attack on the *Königsberg* in line astern. The bombing was highly accurate and the cruiser, having suffered three direct hits and a dozen near misses, exploded and sank. She was the first major warship to be sunk by air attack in war. One Skua was shot down by anti-aircraft fire, which was quite heavy once the Germans had got over their initial surprise, and two more were damaged. It was unfortunate that the *Köln* was no longer in Bergen harbour when the Skuas made their attack; together with the *Bremse* and

some smaller craft, she had put to sea earlier on the orders of Rear-Admiral Schmundt, commanding the Bergen task group. The wreck of the *Königsberg* was refloated in 1943 and dry-docked, but was abandoned and broken up after it capsized in September 1944.

In September 1939, the light cruiser *Nürnberg* was the flagship of Vice-Admiral Densch, commanding the German Naval Reconnaissance Forces, and from 3 September, with other light cruisers, she was active in laying mines in the North Sea. On 12 December 1939, she was attacked by the submarine *Salmon* (Lieutenant-Commander Bickford) and received a torpedo hit in the bow. After repair she returned to active duty in the summer of 1940, first in Norwegian waters and then with the Fleet Training Squadron in the Baltic. In September

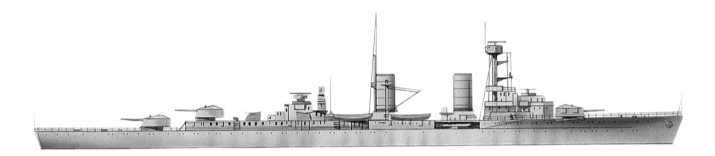

SPECIFICATIONS: *KÖLN*

GENERAL

Ship type: Light cruiser

Entered service: 1929

Fate: Sunk at Wilhelmshaven 30/4/45

MACHINERY

Engine: Diesel

Power: Two-shaft geared turbines

ARMOUR

Belt: 76–100mm (3–4in)

Turrets: 51mm (2in)

ARMAMENT

Eight 15cm (6in) guns; three 8.8cm (3.5in)
and four 37mm (1.5in) AA guns

DIMENSIONS

Length: 150.3m (493ft)

Width: 14.3m (47ft)

Height: 5.34m (17ft 6in)

Displacement: 5690 tonnes (5600 tons)

PERFORMANCE

Speed: 54km/h (29 knots)

1941, she participated in the blockade of the Soviet Baltic Fleet. She saw little action until 13 January 1945, when she carried out defensive mining operations in the Skagerrak, fighting off several attacks by British aircraft. On 9 May she surrendered to the Allies at Copenhagen, alongside the *Prinz Eugen*, and in January 1946 she was turned over to the Soviet Union at Libau, subsequently serving in the Soviet Navy as the *Admiral Makarov*. The light cruisers *Leipzig* and *Köln* also carried out mining operations in the North Sea area during the early weeks of the war, prior to participating in the invasion of Norway. Both were subsequently transferred to the Baltic (the *Köln* after serving in Norway during 1942–43), where they took part in operations against Soviet forces. On 15 October 1944, the *Leipzig* was badly damaged in a collision with the *Prinz Eugen* off Gdynia. The *Köln* herself was bombed and sunk at Wilhelmshaven on 30 April 1945, while the *Leipzig* – having taken part in the evacuation from East Prussia, despite her unseaworthy condition – surrendered to the Allies and was sunk in the North Sea in July 1946, laden with highly lethal canisters of poison gas. The seafaring activities of the original post-World War I German light cruiser, the *Emden*, are described in the Introduction.

ABOVE *The light cruiser* Köln *was used in support of German ground forces fighting against the Russians in the Baltic States in 1944 and also served with the Fleet Training Squadron.*

ABOVE *The light cruiser* Leipzig *after being rammed by the heavy cruiser* Prinz Eugen *off the Hela peninsula in the Baltic, 15 October 1944. The* Leipzig *was badly damaged and her operational career was at an end. She was sunk in the North Sea with a cargo of poison gas in July 1946.*

BELOW *Entering service in 1929, four years before the Nazis came to power, the light cruiser* Karlsrühe *made several foreign cruises as a training ship before the war. She was torpedoed by the British submarine HMS* Truant *on 10 April 1940 and later sunk by a motor torpedo boat off Kristiansand.*

CHAPTER 5

DESTROYER FORCES

Germany completed 40 destroyers, mostly just before the outbreak of World War II. Twenty more were ordered and on the stocks but were mostly abandoned. Of the destroyers that did see operational service, 23 were destroyed in action; others were bombed and sunk in harbour.

The German Navy began World War II with two classes of destroyer; the Diether von Roeder class, comprising six ships, and the Leberecht Maass class of 16. The two classes were similar in size and armament, although the von Roeder class had a superior performance, being capable of 70km/h (38 knots) against the Leberecht Maass's 56km/h (30 knots). Range was better, too; 8987km (4850nm) at 35km/h (19 knots) against 8153km (4400nm).

At the outbreak of war, all German destroyers in the North Sea area were under the operational command of

LEFT *German troops disembarking from a destroyer during the invasion of Norway, 9 April 1940. The German Navy's destroyers played a big part in this operation, but suffered heavy losses at the hands of elements of the Royal Navy's destroyer forces.*

Vice-Admiral Densch's Reconnaissance Forces, and were organised as follows. The 1st Destroyer Flotilla (Captain Meisel) with the *Georg Thiele, Richard Beitzen, Friedrich Ihn, Erich Steinbrinck* and *Friedrich Eckoldt*; the 2nd Destroyer Flotilla (Captain Bonte) with the *Theodor Riedel, Hermann Schoemann, Bruno Heinemann* and *Leberecht Maass*; the 4th Destroyer Flotilla (Commander Bey) with the *Bernd von Arnim, Hans Lody* and *Erich Giese*; and the 5th Destroyer Flotilla (Commander H. Harrmann) with the *Diether von Roeder, Hans Lüdemann, Hermann Künne* and *Karl Galster*. The remaining destroyers – the *Wilhelm Heidkamp, Anton Schmitt, Max Schulz, Paul Jacobi, Wolfgang Zenker* and *Erich Koellner* – were either in the Baltic or were not immediately available for operations.

During September 1939, all destroyers under Densch's command were engaged in laying mine

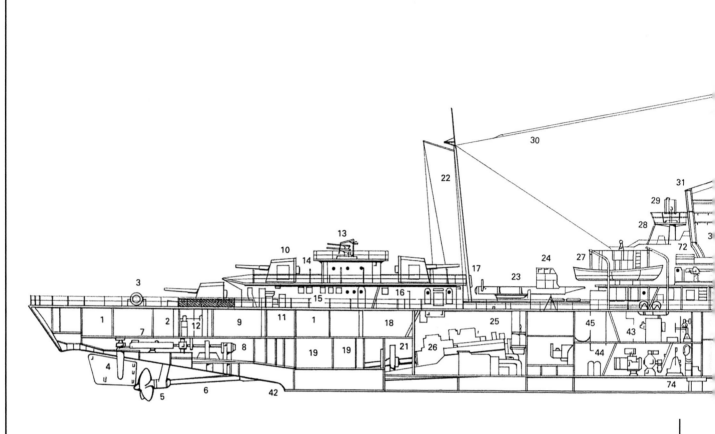

1. Store
2. Auxiliary engine room
3. Capstan
4. Balanced rudder
5. Twin propellers
6. Shaft
7. Steering gear
8. Steering engine
9. Machine shop
10. 127mm (5in) 45-calibre c34 gun
11. Ammunition hoist
12. Turret training engine
13. Four barrelled 2cm AA gun
14. Aft wireless room
15. Wardroom/officers' quarters
16. Sick bay
17. Captain's cabin
18. Engineers' quarters
19. Fuel
20. Wind passage
21. Reduction gear
22. Mainmast
23. Four 533mm torpedo tubes (centre line)
24. Torpedo tube operator's screen

25. Turbine room
26. Turbine
27. Lifeboat
28. Searchlight platform
29. Searchlight
30. Wireless aerial
31. Superheater
32. Funnel cap
33. Funnel chasing
34. Twin 2cm AA guns
35. Launch
36. Derrick
37. Funnel uptake
38. No 1 boiler room
39. No 2 boiler room
40. No 3 boiler room
41. No 4 boiler room
42. Keel
43. Engine room
44. Main engine
45. Fresh water tank
46. Tripod foremast
47. Ladder
48. Lockout position
49. Foretop
50. Warning & gunnery radar

51. Radar room
52. Radio direction finder
53. Target bearing transmitter
54. Bridge
55. Wireless room
56. Control room/chart room
57. Companionway
58. Crew's mess
59. Shell room
60. Ammunition hoist
61. Crew quarters
62. Breakwater
63. Capstan
64. Capstan engine
65. Auxiliary engine/machine shop
66. Foredeck
67. Anchor room
68. Paint store
69. Waterline
70. Extending paravene gear
71. Magazine
72. Ventilators
73. Feed tank to boilers
74. Double bottom

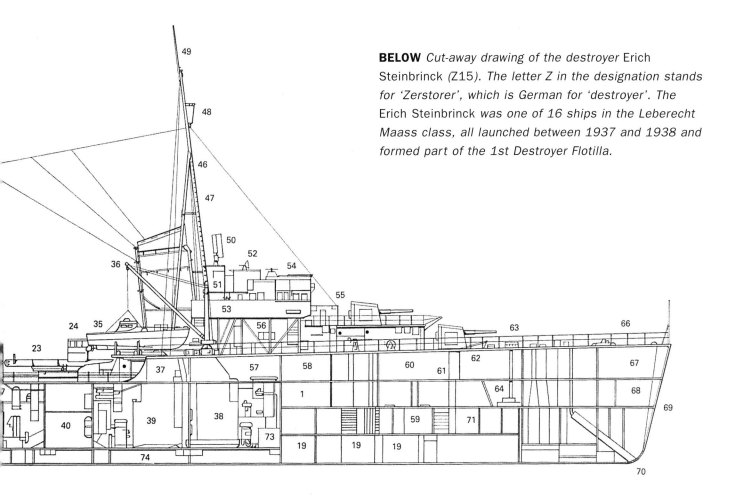

BELOW *Cut-away drawing of the destroyer* Erich Steinbrinck *(Z15). The letter Z in the designation stands for 'Zerstorer', which is German for 'destroyer'. The* Erich Steinbrinck *was one of 16 ships in the Leberecht Maass class, all launched between 1937 and 1938 and formed part of the 1st Destroyer Flotilla.*

SPECIFICATIONS: *ERICH STEINBRINCK*

GENERAL

Ship type: Destroyer

Entered service: 1939

Complement: 315

Fate: Given to USSR as *Pylki* (1946)

MACHINERY

Engine: Diesel

Power: Two-shaft geared turbines

ARMOUR

Belt: 76mm (3in)

Turrets: 51mm (2in)

ARMAMENT

Main: Five 12.7cm (5in) guns

Secondary: Four 37mm (1.5in) AA guns;
eight 53cm (21in) torpedo tubes;
60 mines

DIMENSIONS

Length: 114m (374ft)

Width: 11.3m (37ft)

Height: 2.9m (9ft 6in)

Displacement: 2335 tonnes (2200 tons)

PERFORMANCE

Speed: 56km/h (30 knots)

barrages in the North Sea, and early in October, nine of them took part in a sortie towards the southern coast of Norway in an attempt to draw the British Home Fleet towards a concentration of U-boats. On 17–18 October, six destroyers laid mines in the Humber estuary, with the result that seven ships totalling 26,239 tonnes (25,825 tons) were sunk. Further mining operations in November, this time off the Thames estuary by four destroyers under Captain Bonte, resulted in the sinking of

the British destroyer HMS *Blanche* and 13 merchant vessels totalling 49,510 tonnes (48,728 tons), and on the night of 12–13 December, five destroyers mined the area of the Tyne estuary, with the result that 11 merchant ships of 19,284 tonnes (18,979 tons) were sunk.

Mines, in fact, were the main threat to British shipping in home waters, and for a time the Germans enjoyed a definite advantage through the use of the magnetic mine, detonated by the magnetic field of a vessel passing over it. Such mines accounted for 59,974 tonnes (59,027 tons) of British coastal shipping in September–October 1939, and to compound the problem, the entire British minesweeping service was equipped to deal only with moored contact mines that detonated on impact. A major coup for the Royal Navy was the recovery, on 23 November 1939, of two German magnetic mines from the mud flats at Shoeburyness. Defused and made safe by a gallant Royal Navy team (Lieutenant-Commanders Ouvry and Lewis, CPO Baldwin and AB Vearncombe), they were transported to Portsmouth for detailed examination. Once the magnetic mine's secrets were unlocked, the Admiralty initiated all technical measures to combat it. Before long, a research team under Rear-Admiral W.F. Wake-Walker had devised countermeasures in the form of a so-called degaussing girdle, an electric cable fitted to the hulls of ships to de-magnetize them. Girdles were also fitted to modified Vickers Wellingtons of No 1 General Reconnaissance Unit, RAF Coastal Command, whose task it was to fly low over the sea and detonate the mines through the generation of an electromagnetic field.

These developments came just in time. In November 1939, enemy minelaying became so intensive that only a single channel into the Thames remained open, and in that month mines accounted for 27 ships totalling 122,900 tonnes (120,958 tons). As the official naval historian Captain S.W. Roskill later wrote:

'While awaiting the arrival of the new sweep many extemporised measures were adopted, and together they just succeeded in keeping the east coast traffic moving. Though losses continued on a considerable scale in the New Year, and in the first seven months of war no less than 128 ships totalling 429,899 tons fell victims to mines, we never again had to face as serious a crisis as that of the first autumn.'

The losses, however, were not all one-sided. On 22 February 1940, the German destroyers *Leberecht Maass* and *Max Schultz* were mined and sunk in the North Sea,

BELOW *The destroyer* Leberecht Maass *which was part of the 2nd Destroyer Flotilla commanded by Captain Erich Bonte. Along with the rest of the German Navy's destroyers, the* Leberecht Maass *spent most of its time laying mines in the early months of the war. It was soon to reap what it had sowed.*

SPECIFICATIONS: *LEBERECHT MAASS*

GENERAL	ARMOUR	DIMENSIONS
Ship type: Destroyer	**Belt:** 76mm (3in)	**Length:** 114m (374ft)
Entered service: 1939	**Turrets:** 51mm (2in)	**Width:** 11.3m (37ft)
Complement: 315		**Height:** 2.9m (9ft 6in)
Fate: Sunk by mine 22/2/40	**ARMAMENT**	**Displacement:** 2335 tonnes (2200 tons)
	Main: Five 12.7cm (5in) guns	
MACHINERY	**Secondary:** Four 37mm (1.5in) AA guns;	**PERFORMANCE**
Engine: Diesel	eight 53cm (21in) torpedo tubes;	**Speed:** 56km/h (30 knots)
Power: Two-shaft geared turbines	60 mines	

ABOVE *A Leberecht Maass-class destroyer pictured from the icy deck of the heavy cruiser* Prinz Eugen *in May 1942, during operations in northern waters. On its return to the relative safety of German waters, the naval task force had to beat off strong attacks by RAF torpedo bombers.*

northwest of Borkum, and for the Germans there was worse to come.

In April 1940, 10 destroyers under the command of the newly promoted Commodore Friedrich Bonte formed Task Group One, engaged in the invasion of Norway, their target the northern port of Narvik. Carrying 2000 men of General Dietl's 3rd Mountain Division, they passed unopposed through the narrow waterway between the Lofoten Islands and the Norwegian mainland in the early hours of 9 April. As they entered Ofotfjord on the approach to Narvik, Bonte detached seven destroyers: three to deal with Norwegian forts said to be defending the Ramnes Narrows (in fact there were none), and four to occupy the township of Elvegaard in Herjangsfjord. The remaining three – Bonte's flagship the *Wilhelm Heidkamp*, followed by the *Bernd von Arnim* and *Georg Thiele* – pressed on to Narvik,

sinking the Norwegian defence vessels *Eidsvold* and *Norge* as they entered the harbour.

The small Norwegian garrison was quickly overwhelmed and Bonte redeployed his destroyers, bringing the *Anton Schmitt, Diether von Roeder* and *Hans Lüdemann* into Narvik after they had disembarked their troops. The destroyers ought to have made the return passage to Germany at high speed once their troops were ashore, but before they could do so they needed fuel, and only one of the expected tankers had turned up. Bonte therefore decided to delay the voyage home until the next day, while his destroyers took it in turns to take on fuel. He was not expecting any trouble; the submarine *U51* had reported sighting five British destroyers in Vestfjord at 2022 hours, but had signalled that they were steering southwest, away from the entrance of Ofotfjord. In fact, the British destroyers were already making for Narvik, with orders to 'make certain that no enemy troops land,' in the words of the Admiralty's instructions, or if they had already landed 'to sink or capture enemy ships and land forces if you think you can recapture Narvik from number of enemy present.'

The destroyers, under the command of Captain B.A. Warburton-Lee, were the *Hardy, Hunter, Havock,*

Hotspur and *Hostile* of the 2nd Destroyer Flotilla. Signalling his intention to attack at dawn high water, which would give him the advantage of surprise and enable his ships to pass safely over any mines, Warburton-Lee led his ships slowly in line ahead through Ofotfjord, in visibility reduced by falling snow, and reached the entrance to Narvik harbour without being detected by the enemy. Detaching *Hotspur* and *Hostile* to watch for and neutralise any shore batteries, he took *Hardy* into the harbour at 0430 hours and launched seven torpedoes at shipping in the anchorage. One torpedo ripped through the *Heidkamp*'s plating and exploded in her after-magazine, killing Bonte and most of his sleeping crew. Two more destroyed the *Anton Schmitt*; the other four struck merchant vessels, or missed their targets.

Battle of attrition

Hardy swung round in a tight circle, her 12cm (4.7in) guns firing, as the *Hunter* and *Havock* entered the anchorage in turn. Their torpedoes set the *Hans Ludemann* ablaze and then they turned on the *Diether von Roeder*, assisted by the *Hotspur* and *Hostile*, which had found no shore batteries to engage, and reduced her to a burning wreck that just managed to reach the shore, where her captain beached her. Only one German destroyer, the *Hermann Künne*, escaped the attack, and even then she was disabled, her engines damaged by the explosions of the torpedoes which sank the *Schmitt*.

The British destroyers withdrew from the harbour and made their way down Ofotfjord at 15 knots, still with plenty of ammunition left. As they passed Herangsfjord to starboard, the German destroyers *Wolfgang Zenker,*

ABOVE *The destroyer* Leberecht Maass (Z1) *seen before the outbreak of war. This class of German destroyer was the first to have torpedo tubes in quadruple mounts. From 1944, the anti-aircraft armament was increased. She was mined and sunk in the North Sea, off Borkum, on 22 February 1940.*

Erich Giese and *Erich Koellner* were seen emerging from it, and both sides opened fire, the British ships increasing speed to 56km/h (30 knots). Ahead of them, two more German destroyers, the *Georg Thiele* and *Bernd von Arnim*, crept out of Ballangenfjord into the British warships' path, trapping them between two forces. In the savage fight that ensued, HMS *Hardy* received the full weight of fire from the *Thiele* and *Arnim*. With her captain mortally wounded and her steering gear shattered, she grounded on some rocks 275m (300 yards) from shore. About 170 of her crew struggled ashore, taking Warburton-Lee with them, lashed to a Carley Float. He died just as they pulled him from the water.

Lieutenant-Commander L. de Villiers in HMS *Hunter* now led the British line. Raked by shells and burning, *Hunter* lost all power. Close behind her, Lieutenant-Commander H.F. Layman in HMS *Hotspur* gave urgent orders to take avoiding action, but at that moment a German shell cut the steering controls and *Hotspur*'s bow ripped into the helpless destroyer in front. Both ships now came under heavy fire. With shells bursting all around, Layman managed to make his way from the bridge to the after-steering position, and after much effort succeeded in extricating his badly damaged ship from the sinking *Hunter*. The other two British destroyers, *Havock* and

Hostile, came to *Hotspur*'s rescue, engaging the *Thiele* and *Arnim* as the latter ran down the fjord in the opposite direction, both seriously damaged. The German vessels vanished in the murk, leaving the British warships free to continue their dash for the open sea. Of the *Hunter*'s crew of nearly 200, 50 men were rescued from the waters.

It was not quite over. As the British destroyers headed seawards, they sighted a large German merchant ship, the *Rauenfels*, entering the fjord. Two shells compelled her crew to abandon ship; two more caused her to blow up. The Germans might still be in possession of Narvik, but their surviving destroyers could no longer depend on fresh supplies of ammunition with which to replenish their dwindling stocks.

So ended the action that came to be known as the first battle of Narvik. It had left the Germans with two destroyers sunk, three so badly damaged as to be unseaworthy, one (the *Lüdemann*) with a flooded magazine and another with her engines out of action. Set against the loss of two British destroyers, it was a notable victory, and one that earned Captain Warburton-Lee the award of a posthumous Victoria Cross.

Two days later, other German destroyers, operating in support of Task Group 2 at Trondheim, had a narrow escape. On 11 April, Admiral Forbes, C-in-C British Home Fleet, authorised a sortie towards Trondheim with the battleships *Rodney*, *Valiant* and *Warspite*, the carrier *Furious* and the heavy cruisers *Berwick*, *Devonshire* and *York*. The carrier launched a strike of 18 Fairey Swordfish of Nos 816 and 818 Squadrons against the *Hipper*, reported to be at Trondheim, but the German cruiser had departed for Germany with the destroyer *Friedrich*

Eckoldt. Three others, the *Paul Jacobi*, *Theodor Riedel* and *Bruno Heidemann* were still at Trondheim awaiting the arrival of their tanker and these were attacked, but the water was too shallow for the air-dropped torpedoes to function properly and they exploded harmlessly on the bottom.

The Admiralty, meanwhile, was anxious to finish the job begun by Captain Warburton-Lee's destroyers at Narvik on 10 April, and on 13 April, the destroyers *Bedouin*, *Cossack*, *Eskimo*, *Forester*, *Foxhound*, *Hero*, *Icarus*, *Kimberley* and *Punjabi*, covered by the *Warspite*, were sent to comb the surrounding fjords for the eight surviving German vessels. The *Warspite*'s Swordfish floatplane sighted the submarine *U64* and sank her, while the destroyers fell on the enemy ships. The Germans were no match for the British force, and all were destroyed or scuttled. Three British destroyers were damaged, two seriously. Swordfish from the *Furious* also took part in this second battle of Narvik, but scored no successes and lost two of their number. After this, the carrier remained at Tromso for several days to provide air reconnaissance facilities after the fleet returned to Scapa for replenishment, suffering damage from a near miss during an air attack. In all, she was in action for 14 days, during which she lost nine Swordfish, with three aircrew

BELOW *The destroyer* Hans Lody (Z10). *Launched in 1938, she was part of the 4th Destroyer Flotilla, commanded by Commander Bey. The* Hans Lody *survived the war and was seized by the Royal Navy as war booty in 1945, being allocated the penant number R38. She was broken up in 1949.*

SPECIFICATIONS: *Z23*

GENERAL

Ship type: Destroyer

Entered service: 1940

Complement: 321

Fate: Sunk at La Pallice 21/8/44

MACHINERY

Engine: Diesel

Power: Two-shaft geared turbines

ARMOUR

Belt: 76mm (3in)

Turrets: 51mm (2in)

ARMAMENT

Main: Four 15cm (6in) guns

Secondary: Various AA guns; eight 53cm
(21in) torpedo tubes; 60 mines

DIMENSIONS

Length: 119m (390ft)

Width: 12.2m (40ft)

Height: 3m (10ft)

Displacement: 2335 tonnes (2200 tons)

PERFORMANCE

Speed: 70km/h (38 knots)

killed and nine wounded. All the remaining aircraft of her air group were damaged to some extent.

By the middle of April 1940, therefore, the German destroyer force had been reduced to 10 ships out of the original 22. Twelve more ships, designated *Z23-Z34*, had already been laid down, but the first would not be ready for service until early in 1941; in the meantime, Captain Bey's much reduced destroyer force was occupied mainly with minelaying activities, or with escorting other minelaying craft in the North Sea and English Channel areas. On 17 October 1940, Bey led the destroyers *Hans Lody, Karl Galster, Friedrich Ihn* and *Erich Steinbrink* in a sortie towards the western exit of the Bristol Channel; there was a confused engagement with British cruisers and destroyers, both sides eventually breaking off without sustaining damage. In a second sortie, on the night of 24-25 November, the German destroyers sank two small freighters off Plymouth, and on the night of 28–29 November, the German warships sank two more small vessels and damaged the British destroyer *Javelin* in the same area. During this engagement HMS *Javelin* was hit by two torpedoes, which blew off her bow and stern and detonated the ammunition in her magazine, destroying

ABOVE *The 12 destroyers of the Z23 class were all launched between 1940 and 1942. They served mostly with the German Navy's 8th Destroyer Flotilla. They were popularly known as 'Narviks' and were mainly based in Norway. Six were lost in action, a loss proportional to that suffered by other German destroyer units.*

her superstructure as well as killing three officers and 43 ratings. Remarkably, she remained afloat and was towed into harbour. She eventually returned to operations and went on to survive the war.

Enemy mines accounted for the highest proportion of British shipping losses in the closing months of 1940. Of the 42 Royal Navy vessels lost in the Channel area between 1 September and the end of the year, 28 were sunk by mines.

The first operational sortie by the first of the new class of destroyer, *Z23*, was on 19 May 1941, when she joined the *Friedrich Eckoldt* and *Hans Lody* in escorting the battleship *Bismarck* on the first stage of her ill-fated journey from the Baltic to the North Atlantic. The new destroyers were similar to the pre-war craft, although their endurance was progressively increased; the last five of the batch, *Z30–Z34*, had an endurance of 10,933km (5900nm) at 35km/h (19 knots). In July 1941, the 6th Destroyer Flotilla under Captain Schulze-Hinrichs, comprising the *Hans Lody, Karl Galster, Hermann Schoemann, Friedrich Eckoldt* and *Richard Beitzen*, was transferred to Kirkenes in northern Norway for operations off the Kola peninsula, and soon began to register successes against Soviet coastal traffic. Later in the year the 8th Destroyer Flotilla, comprising the *Z23, Z24, Z25* and *Z27* under Capt Pönitz, was also transferred to Norway for operations off Kola, and on 17 December it fought an action against the British minesweepers *Hazard* and *Speedy*, which had emerged from the Kola Inlet to meet the inbound Convoy PQ6 and which the Germans mistook for Soviet destroyers. *Speedy* was damaged by four shell hits, and the enemy ships broke off the engagement on the approach of the British heavy cruiser *Kent* and two Soviet destroyers.

In waters closer to home, the destroyer *Bruno Heinemann (Z8)* was sunk on 25 January 1942 by a mine laid off the French coast between Ushant and Boulogne by the Royal Navy minelayers *Welshman* and *Manxman*. Three weeks later, on 12 February, six destroyers – the *Z25, Z29, Friedrich Ihn, Hermann Schoemann, Paul Jacobi* and *Richard Beitzen* – passed through the

ABOVE *The destroyer Z24 was bombed and sunk by de Havilland Mosquito aircraft of the Royal Air Force at Le Verdon on 25 April 1944. Note the radar array just in front of the mast. Z24 was one of the destroyers deployed to the Channel area to meet the threat of the anticipated Allied invasion.*

BELOW *The Z-class destroyer Z25 survived the war, unlike many of her sister ships, and was taken over by the Royal Navy in May 1945. She subsequently served with the French Navy as the* Hoche, *before being broken up in 1956. The photograph shows her as she appeared in French service.*

Channel unscathed, escorting the *Scharnhorst*, *Gneisenau* and *Prinz Eugen* in their breakout from Brest.

The *Z25*, *Hermann Schoemann* and *Richard Beitzen* returned to Norway later in the month, together with the *Friedrich Ihn*. On 20 March 1942, German naval strength in Norway was further augmented with the arrival at Trondheim of the heavy cruiser *Admiral Hipper*, accompanied by the destroyers *Z24*, *Z26* and *Z30* and the torpedo-boats *T15*, *T16* and *T17*. The enemy now had a formidable striking force of aircraft, warships and submarines in the theatre, and convoy losses inevitably began to mount. Between 27 and 31 March, PQ13 became split up due to bad weather; two of its ships were sunk by the Ju 88s of I/KG 30, operating from Banak, three by U-boats, and one by the destroyer *Z26* (Commander von Berger), which was herself sunk by the cruiser *Trinidad*. The cruiser was then hit by one of her own torpedoes, which went out of control; the *U585* closed in to attack her, but was sunk by the destroyer *Fury*. The destroyers *Z24* and *Z25*, meanwhile, closing in to rescue 96 crewmen from the sinking *Z26*, inflicted damage on the British ship *Eclipse* before withdrawing. The remaining 13 ships of PQ13 reached Murmansk, but two were sunk by air attack on 3 April.

Operations against the convoys

Convoy PQ14 (8–21 April) ran into ice floes in thick fog and 16 of its 24 vessels had to return to Iceland. One was sunk by the *U403*. PQ15 (26 April–7 May), a large convoy of 50 ships under heavy Anglo-American escort, had two vessels sunk by air attack and one damaged (this

ABOVE *The 'Narvik' destroyer Z31, launched in 1942. Like the Z25, she was allocated to Royal Navy at the end of World War II as war reparation and afterwards handed over to the French Navy, in which she saw some years' service as the* Marceau. *Also like the Z25, she was broken up in 1956.*

ship, the *Jutland*, was later sunk by the *U251*). QP11, a homeward-bound convoy, was attacked by destroyers and U-boats. Two British destroyers, the *Forester* and *Foresight*, were badly damaged in an engagement with the German destroyers *Z24* and *Z25*; the battleship *King George V* rammed and sank the destroyer *Punjabi* in a snowstorm and was herself damaged by the latter's exploding depth charges; and, to add to a catalogue of woe, the Polish submarine *Jastrzab*, a long way from her position on the flank of the convoy, was sunk by the Norwegian-manned destroyer *St Albans* and the minesweeper *Seagull*.

On 1 May 1942, during these operations against the convoys, the *Hermann Schoemann* was badly damaged by gunfire from the cruiser HMS *Edinburgh* and was abandoned the next day. The *Edinburgh*, already hit by a U-boat torpedo, was hit by another from either the *Z24* or *Z25* with the result that she was also abandoned and had to be sunk by other British warships.

On 16 May the *Paul Jacobi* and *Z25* sailed from Trondheim as part of the escort for the *Prinz Eugen*, en route to Kiel after being damaged by a torpedo in February. They arrived on 18 May, having beaten off fierce

British air attacks en route, and were consequently absent from the Arctic when, a month later, the entire available destroyer force in Norway was assembled for operations against the ill-starred Convoy PQ17. The destroyers *Richard Beitzen, Friedrich Eckoldt, Karl Galster, Friedrich Ihn, Hans Lody, Theodor Riedel, Erich Steinbrinck, Z24, Z27, Z28, Z29* and *Z30* left their bases at Narvik and Trondheim and converged on Altenfjord, but the *Hans Lody, Karl Galster* and *Theodor Riedel* were put out of action almost immediately when, on 3 July, they ran aground in company with the *Lützow*. The destruction of the convoy was left to U-boats and aircraft.

Mine-laying activities

During September and October, the German destroyers took advantage of the sudden cessation of convoy traffic to lay mines in Soviet waters. Early in November, warships of Captain Schemmel's 5th Destroyer Flotilla – the *Friedrich Eckoldt, Richard Beitzen, Z27* and *Z30* – set out to intercept 13 Soviet ships sailing independently from Reykjavik, Iceland, to Murmansk and Archangel. The tanker *Donbass* and the submarine-chaser BO78 were sunk by *Z27*.

The German destroyers' next surface action against British warships took place in December 1942, during the Battle of the Barents Sea. All the vessels of the 5th Destroyer Flotilla were involved in this action: they were the *Friedrich Eckoldt* (Commander Bachmann), *Z29* (Commander Rechel), *Richard Beitzen* (Commander von Davidson), *Theodor Riedel* (Commander Riede), *Z30* (Commander Kaiser) and *Z31* (Commander Alberts). In the course of the battle (described in Chapter Four) the *Friedrich Eckoldt* was sunk by the cruiser HMS *Sheffield*.

Meanwhile, the *Z24* had left the Arctic to reinforce

the French-based 8th Destroyer Flotilla (Captain Erdmenger), and on 28 March 1943, she joined *Z23, Z32* and *Z37* in escorting the Italian blockade-runner *Pietro Orseleo* on the first leg of her voyage from the Gironde to Japan. On 1 April, they beat off RAF torpedo-bombers, shooting five down, but the Italian ship was torpedoed by the US submarine *Shad* and had to be towed back to the Gironde on the following day. On 9 April, heavy air attacks also forced the return of another Italian blockade-runner, the *Himalaya*, despite a strong destroyer escort.

From June 1943, destroyers were also used to escort U-boats traversing the Bay of Biscay on the surface in groups of four or five, to provide mutual fire support against Allied aircraft. From now on, this was to be the most important area of operations for the surviving German destroyers; although they were still active in the Arctic in the latter half of 1943 – the 5th and 6th Destroyer Flotillas took part in the bombardment of Spitzbergen in September, for example, and the 4th Destroyer Flotilla (Captain Johannesson) formed the destroyer screen for the battle-cruiser *Scharnhorst* during her final action in December off North Cape – the U-boats and aircraft would assume increasing responsibility for the Arctic war.

There were some hard-fought actions in the Biscay area during the closing weeks of 1943, as the 8th Destroyer Flotilla joined other forces in beating off

BELOW *The German Z class destroyers were formidable fighting ships, but by 1943–44, they were no match for the weight of Allied air power directed against them. Three were sunk by air attack, and several severely damaged. Like most German equipment, their quality was of limited value against overwhelming odds.*

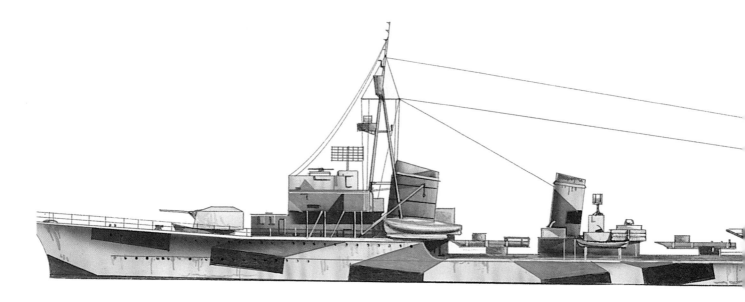

SPECIFICATIONS: *Z37*

GENERAL

Ship type: Destroyer

Entered service: 1940

Complement: 321

Fate: Scuttled at Bordeaux 1944

MACHINERY

Engine: Diesel

Power: Two-shaft geared turbines

ARMOUR

Belt: 76mm (3in)

Turrets: 51mm (2in)

ARMAMENT

Main: Four 15cm (6in) guns

Secondary: Various AA guns; eight 53cm
(21in) torpedo tubes; 60 mines

DIMENSIONS

Length: 119m (390ft)

Width: 12.2m (40ft)

Height: 3m (10ft)

Displacement: 2335 tonnes (2200 tons)

PERFORMANCE

Speed: 70km/h (38 knots)

attacks on homeward-bound blockade-runners. In one of them, the flotilla commander, Captain Erdmenger, was killed alongside Commander Günther Schulz when the destroyer *Z27* was sunk in a gun engagement with the British cruisers *Glasgow* and *Enterprise* on 28 December.

Early in 1944, the 6th Destroyer Flotilla (*Z25*, *Z28*, *Z35* and *Z39*, under Captain Kothe) moved to the Gulf of Finland, shelling Soviet shore positions and renewing old minefields. The destroyer *Z39* was severely damaged by air attack during these operations in June. In August, the *Z25*, *Z28*, *Z35* and *Z36* joined the *Prinz Eugen* in shelling Soviet troops who had broken through on the Gulf of Riga; during similar operations in October the *Z28* was damaged by a bomb hit. In December the 6th Flotilla lost the *Z35* and *Z36*, which sank after hitting mines.

Meanwhile, the 8th Destroyer Flotilla, now under the command of Captain von Bechtolsheim, continued to be active in the Channel area, and on the night of 8–9 June 1944, following the Allied invasion of Normandy, its

ABOVE *The destroyer Z37 displaying the unusual camouflage scheme adopted whilst serving in the Baltic. Z37 was scuttled at Bordeaux in August 1944 to avoid capture by the Allies. Her sister, Z38, was taken over by the Royal Navy before being broken up in 1949.*

warships set out from Brest to attack the invasion forces. They were intercepted by British destroyers; the former Dutch destroyer *ZH1*, now in German service, was sunk by torpedoes from HMS *Ashanti*, and *Z32* was beached and blown up after a gun duel with HMS *Haida* and HMS *Huron*. On 21 August, the *Z23* was destroyed in an air attack at La Pallice, while four days later RAF bombers sank the *Z24* at Le Verdon. Another destroyer, *Z37*, was scuttled at Bordeaux on 24 August. These losses effectively spelt the end of operations by the 8th Flotilla.

From the end of 1944, German destroyer operations were focused on the Baltic, supporting the final evacuations from East Prussia. On 6 March 1945, the *Z28*

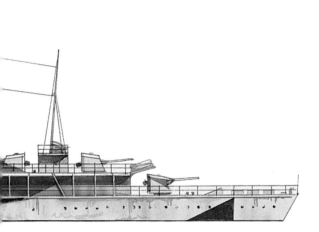

The *Theodor Riedel* (Z6) also went to France from Britain as the *Kleber*; she was not scrapped until 1958. The Hans Lody (Z10) went to the Royal Navy under the pennant number R38, and was broken up in 1949, while the *Friedrich Ihn* (Z14) and Erich Steinbrinck (Z15) went to the USSR as the *Zorki* and *Pylki* respectively.

The *Z25* went first to Britain, then to France as the *Hoche*; she was broken up in 1956. The *Z29*, taken on charge by the USA, was scuttled in the Skagerrak in December 1946 with explosives on board. The *Z30*, assigned to Britain, was blown up in explosive experiments; the *Z31* went to France as the *Marceau*, being broken up in 1956; while the *Z33* went to the USSR as the *Proworny*. Finally, the *Z38* went to the Royal Navy as the *Nonsuch*, being scrapped in 1949, while the *Z39*, assigned to the US Navy as DD939, was used as spares for the German destroyers taken over by France.

Sixteen more German destroyers (Z42 to Z56) were laid down in World War II but they were never completed.

was bombed and sunk at Sassnitz; on 8 May the destroyers *Karl Galster, Friedrich Ihn, Hans Lody, Theodor Riedel*, Z25, Z38, and Z39 surrendered. Of the German destroyers that survived World War II, the *Karl Galster* (Z20) went to the Soviet Navy as the *Protschny*. The *Richard Beitzen* (Z4) went to Britain, and was broken up in 1947. The *Paul Jacobi* (Z5) also went to Britain initially, but in February 1946 she was assigned to the French Navy as the *Desaix*; she was broken up in 1951.

BELOW *The Z40 class destroyers were authorised in 1939, but cancelled in the following year. Work on a modified design was resumed in 1941, when they were reclassified as Spahkreuzer (scout cruisers). All three of these vessels were broken up on the stocks in 1943.*

SPECIFICATIONS: Z40 (SP1)

GENERAL

Ship type: Scout cruiser

Entered service: Abandoned

Complement: Not known

Fate: Broken up in 1943

MACHINERY

Engine: Diesel

Power: Two-shaft geared turbines

ARMOUR

Not known

ARMAMENT

Main: Six 15cm (6in) guns

Secondary: Two 8.8cm (3.5in), eight 37mm (1.5in), 12 20mm (0.78in) AA guns; ten 53cm (21in) torpedo tubes; 140 mines

DIMENSIONS

Length: 146.4m (480ft)

Width: 14.6m (48ft)

Height: 4.27m (14ft)

Displacement: 4613 tonnes (4540 tons)

PERFORMANCE

Speed: 66km/h (36 knots)

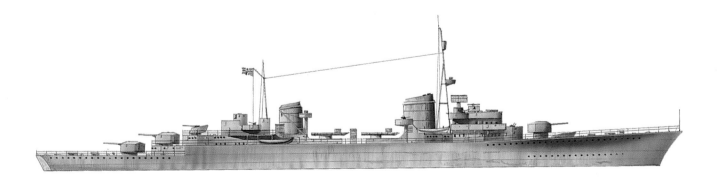

CHAPTER 6

TORPEDO BOATS: THE NAVY'S 'MAIDS OF ALL WORK'

Germany's first twelve torpedo boats were completed in 1926–29 and, in effect, formed the nucleus of a reborn German navy, which held them in considerable affection. In addition to the German vessels, 26 boats were taken over from Italy in 1943 and served in the Mediterranean. Nine more were also captured from France.

One of the most important and versatile classes of ship used by the German Navy in World War II was the torpedo boat. The concept of this type of craft was well-proven; in fact, Admiral von Tirpitz had laid down the groundwork for its operational use

LEFT *The wartime German caption reported that this photograph shows the crew of a torpedo boat signalling to a damaged U-boat, which they have been ordered to escort into harbour. With their considerable armament, T-boats made excellent escort vessels.*

long before the previous war, the main aim being to deliver massed torpedo attacks on an enemy fleet.

The first 12 torpedo boats to be built between the wars were laid down in 1924 and completed in 1926–29. They were the *Wolf*, *Iltis* (Polecat), *Jaguar*, *Leopard*, *Luchs* (Lynx) and *Tiger* of the 'Wolf' class; and the *Möwe* (Seagull), *Albatros*, *Falke* (Falcon), *Greif* (Griffin), *Kondor* and *Seeadler* (Sea Eagle) in the Möwe class. With a displacement of around 945 tonnes (930 tons), the vessels were powered by two-shaft geared turbines and were capable of 61km/h (33 knots). All were armed with six

53cm (21in) torpedo tubes, three 10.4cm (4.1in) guns and four 20mm (0.79in) anti-aircraft guns. They carried a complement of 129. Twenty-one more torpedo boats were also ordered and launched between 1939 and 1942; these were of roughly similar displacement, but had variations in armament, the emphasis being on anti-aircraft weaponry.

Early casualties

Of the 12 original boats, the *Tiger* became an early casualty, being sunk in a collision with the destroyer *Max Schulz* (Z3) off the Danish island of Bornholm on 25 August 1939, while the *Albatros* was beached in Oslofjord after being damaged by coastal artillery on 10 April 1940, during the invasion of Norway, an operation in which all the torpedo boats were involved. A third boat, the *Leopard*, was sunk in a collision with the minelayer *Preussen* in the Skaggerak on 30 April 1940, and the *Luchs* was torpedoed and sunk in the North Sea on 26 July by the British submarine *Swordfish*.

The losses were made good by the deployment of the first of the new T-boats, which were assigned to the 2nd

ABOVE *German torpedo boats in line astern.* Greif *is in the lead, followed by* Möwe. *Many of the original boats served with the 5th Flotilla, which was based at Cherbourg on the French coast and saw considerable success against British shipping in the English Channel in the early months of World War II.*

TB Flotilla under Commander Riede, the survivors of the Wolf and Möwe classes being grouped in the 5th TB Flotilla (Commander Henne). While the British strove to disrupt German invasion plans, the enemy torpedo boats were extremely active in the Channel area during September and October 1940, laying more minefields to protect the flanks of their projected cross-Channel invasion routes and also making hit-and-run sorties against British shipping. One particularly successful sortie was undertaken on the night of 11–12 October by the German 5th Flotilla from Cherbourg, comprising the torpedo boats *Greif, Kondor, Falke, Seeadler* and *Wolf*. They sank the armed trawlers *Listrac* and *Warwick Deeping* with gunfire and torpedoes, and shortly afterwards destroyed the Free French submarine chasers

CH6 and *CH7*, manned by mixed French and Polish crews. The German ships withdrew safely; although they were engaged by the British destroyers *Jackal*, *Jaguar*, *Jupiter*, *Kelvin* and *Kipling*, the latter achieved nothing more spectacular than several near misses.

Two of the new German vessels became war casualties in 1940. In September, the *T3* was bombed and sunk at Le Havre; she was later raised, repaired and brought back into service, only to be mined and sunk north of Hela, in the Baltic, on 14 March 1945 in company with *T5*. On 7 November 1940, *T6* was mined and sunk in the North Sea; and on 8 January 1941, the *Wolf* was lost after striking a mine off Dunkirk.

Although minelaying remained the torpedo boats' main occupation, with occasional offensive forays into British coastal waters, from mid-1941 they were increasingly employed on escort duty, as German convoys in the Channel and North Sea areas became subjected to heavier attacks by the RAF and by the Royal

BELOW *The torpedo boat* Iltis *wallowing in a heavy sea.* Iltis *was one of the Wolf class boats which proved highly effective vessels for the German Navy. She was sunk off Boulogne on 13 May 1942 in an engagement with a force of British MTBs. Her captain, Lieutenant-Commander Jacobsen, was among those lost.*

Navy's coastal forces. On 12 February 1942, the 2nd TB Flotilla (Commander Erdmann), comprising the *T2*, *T4*, *T5*, *T11* and *T12* from Le Havre, the 3rd TB Flotilla (Commander Wilcke) with the *T13*, *T15*, *T16* and *T17* from Dunkirk, and the 5th TB Flotilla (Commander Schmidt) from Boulogne with the *Seeadler*, *Falke*, *Kondor*, *Iltis* and *Jaguar*, provided an important component of the naval force escorting the *Scharnhorst*, *Gneisenau* and *Prinz Eugen* in their dash through the English Channel. The *Jaguar* was damaged by air attack during this operation.

As the summer progressed, there were frequent skirmishes between opposing coastal forces, with destroyers, torpedo boats and light craft carrying out offensive hit-and-run attacks on enemy coastal traffic. One notable action took place on the night of 14–15 May, when the German raider *Stier* passed through the Channel en route for the Gironde, escorted by the torpedo boats *Kondor*, *Falke*, *Iltis*, *Seeadler* and 16 motor minesweepers. The force was heavily shelled by the Dover batteries and attacked by MTBs, the *Iltis* and *Seeadler* both being sunk with heavy loss of life. The rest escaped, despite attempts by British destroyers to intercept them en route; the British naval forces lost *MTB220* in this action.

Towards the end of 1942, the first of a new class of German torpedo boats made their appearance. There

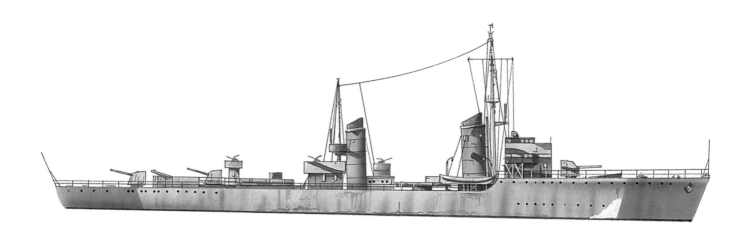

SPECIFICATIONS: *T24*

GENERAL

Ship type: Torpedo boat

Entered service: 1928

Complement: 129

Fate: Sunk by mine 8/1/41

MACHINERY

Engine: Diesel

Power: Two-shaft geared turbines

ARMOUR

Belt: 51cm (2in)

ARMAMENT

Main: Three 105mm (4in) or 127mm (5in) guns

Secondary: Four 20mm (0.78in) AA guns; six 53cm (21in) torpedo tubes

DIMENSIONS

Length: 92.9m (304ft)

Width: 11.6m (28ft)

Height: 2.7m (9ft)

Displacement: 948 tonnes (933 tons)

PERFORMANCE

Speed: 61km/h (33 knots)

ABOVE *Initially classed as destroyers, the Möwe class torpedo boats saw considerable action in the Channel. Six were built, together with six of the Wolf class, and all were lost in action. They were armed mainly for action against surface warships rather than submarines or aircraft.*

were 15 vessels in all, designated *T22-T36*, and they became known as the 'Elbing' class because they were built in the Schichau yard there. Displacing 1315 tonnes (1294 tons) they were powered by two-shaft geared turbines that gave them a top speed of 61km/h (33 knots) and they had an endurance of 9265km (5000nm) at 35km/h (19 knots). They were armed with four 10.4cm (4.1in) guns, four 37mm and nine 20mm anti-aircraft guns and six 53cm (21in) torpedo tubes; their complement was 198.

The 'Elbings' featured prominently on escort operations during 1943, and were involved in a particularly famous sortie in October 1943, when five boats of the 4th TB Flotilla (*T22*, *T23*, *T25*, *T26* and *T27*) under Commander Kohlauf were assigned to escort the German

blockade-runner *Münsterland*, making a fast passage through the English Channel with a cargo of rubber and strategic metals. British warships set out to intercept her, and the light cruiser HMS *Charybdis* made radar contact with the enemy force off Ushant at 0130 hours on 21 October. Her accompanying destroyers also made contact at about the same time, but no information as to the probable size and composition of the enemy force was exchanged.

By this time the Germans were aware of the British warships approaching to intercept them, and the outer screen of torpedo boats obtained a visual sighting on the *Charybdis*, which was seen turning to port. The leading Elbing, *T23*, immediately launched a full salvo of six torpedoes at her. At 0145 hours, the cruiser opened fire with starshell, and her lookouts at once sighted two torpedo tracks heading towards her port side. One, or possibly both, torpedoes struck home and *Charybdis* came to a halt, listing heavily to port.

By now the other German torpedo boats had joined in the action, firing several more torpedoes at the British destroyers coming up behind the stricken cruiser.

RIGHT *Checking torpedoes before loading in a German store at a base on the Atlantic coast, in May 1943. The German Navy experienced constant problems with its torpedoes, which often failed to detonate or exploded prematurely and therefore harmlessly.*

Charybdis was hit again, while a torpedo launched by *T22* struck HMS *Limbourne*. The cruiser sank very quickly, and despite determined attempts to save her, *Limbourne* was also beyond redemption. She was sunk by torpedoes from the *Talybont* and *Rocket*, which returned to Plymouth with the other surviving destroyers.

The action had cost two warships, the lives of 581 officers and ratings, and had achieved nothing. Thanks to the action of the German torpedo boats, the *Münsterland* escaped unscathed, and the next morning air reconnaissance revealed her at Cherbourg and the five Elbings at St Malo. The freighter was subsequently

BELOW *The German torpedo boat* Tiger *struggling through inclement weather in the English Channel. The* Tiger *was an early casualty for the German Navy, being sunk in a collision with the destroyer* Max Schultz (Z3), *north of the Danish island of Bornholm, just before the outbreak of World War II.*

attacked by RAF Typhoon and Whirlwind fighter-bombers through flak described by one pilot as 'a horizontal rainstorm painted red'. Two Whirlwinds out of 12 were shot down and two more crashed on returning to base. The Typhoons lost three aircraft out of eight, but the *Münsterland* was damaged and her progress delayed. She eventually reached Boulogne, where she was again damaged by air attack. Her story came to an end on 20 January 1944, when she ran aground in fog west of Cap Blanc Nez and was shelled to pieces by the Dover gun batteries.

Two of the Elbings involved in this action, *T25* and *T26*, were sunk in the Bay of Biscay on 28 December 1943, by the British cruisers *Glasgow* and *Enterprise*. Against smaller warships, however, the Elbings proved very effective escort vessels, and continued to cause the British serious problems in the Channel area until the Royal Navy adopted new tactics in April 1944. These involved the use of the cruisers *Bellona* and *Black Prince* in the role of command ships, using their radar to direct destroyers of the newly formed 10th Flotilla on to enemy targets and then maintaining a constant plot of the action, using their long-range guns to engage the enemy force and illuminating it constantly with starshells while the destroyers closed in. The tactics worked well, and on 26 April they resulted in the sinking of the *T28*, two more torpedo boats – *T24* and *T27* – being badly damaged and forced to seek shelter in Morlaix. They broke out on the night of 28–29 April and were intercepted off Brieux by the Tribal class destroyers *Haida* and *Athebaskan*. The Germans fired 12 torpedoes at their pursuers and *Athebaskan* was hit, sinking at 0442 hours, but *T27* was further damaged by shells from the *Haida* and ran aground, to be finished off later by MTBs.

The end of the T-boats

It was air attack, however, that sowed the real seeds of destruction among the German torpedo boat flotillas in the build-up to the Allied invasion of Normandy and its immediate aftermath. Of the originals, the *Greif* was bombed and sunk in the Seine estuary on 24 May 1944; the *Jaguar*, *Falke* and *Möwe* were all destroyed by air attack at Le Havre on 15 June; and the last of them, the *Kondor*, was also bombed and sunk at Le Havre on 28 June.

Of the earlier T-class boats, *T15* was bombed and sunk at Kiel on 13 December 1943, while *T2* and *T7* suffered the same fate at Bremen on 29 July 1944. T18 was sunk by air attack in the Baltic on 17 September 1944, while

BELOW *The Möwe class torpedo boat Albatros was one of the vessels detailed to escort the German task force landing troops at Oslo during the invasion of Norway. Another early casualty of the war, she was damaged by coastal artillery and beached on 10 April 1940. She was subsequently scrapped.*

ABOVE *A German convoy off the coast of Norway in June 1943, under the protection of torpedo boats. By this time, German coastal convoys were beginning to suffer from the attentions of RAF Coastal Command's newly formed Strike Wings.*

T10 was destroyed in an air raid at Gdynia on 18 December. All the surviving boats were concentrated in the Baltic, where they took part in evacuating troops and civilians from areas being overrun by Soviet forces. On 10 April 1945, the *T1* went down in an air attack on Kiel, and the *T8* and *T9* were scuttled there on 3 May. The *T13* was destroyed by air attack in the Skagerrak on 10 April 1945, while the *T16* was badly damaged in an air raid on Frederikshavn, Denmark, on 13 April.

Apart from the T24, which was sunk by air attack at Le Verdon in August 1944, the Elbing boats suffered their last losses of the war in the Baltic. The *T22, T30, T32, T34* and *T36* all sank after hitting mines, while the *T31* was torpedoed and sunk by Soviet light forces. A few boats

survived the war to be apportioned among the Allied powers.

Still larger and more powerful classes of torpedo boat would have entered service had the war gone on longer. Fifteen ships of 1517 tonnes (1493 tons), designated *T37-T51*, were either newly launched or still on the stocks at the war's end; all were scuttled or destroyed. Another batch of 12 ships (*T61-T72*) of 1962 tonnes (1931 tons) was envisaged; 15 of these were cancelled and the rest were either bombed on their stocks or broken up.

In addition to the vessels mentioned above, 41 torpedo boats belonging to other nations were taken over by the German Navy. Of these, 26 were Italian, seized when Italy capitulated in September 1943. The rest were Norwegian or French. The four Norwegian vessels were all returned intact to their parent country at the end of the war; the 37 Italian and French ships were used in the Mediterranean theatre, where 26 were sunk in action or by bombing raids in harbour and the rest scuttled.

CHAPTER 7

S-BOATS: THE CHALLENGE IN THE CHANNEL

After the seizure of naval bases in France and the Low Countries in the summer of 1940, German Schnellboote (S-boats) – fast, heavily armed motor torpedo boats – presented a serious threat to British convoys. They were known to the British as E-boats, the 'E' standing simply for 'Enemy'.

Of all the German Navy's attack craft used during World War II, the Schnellboote – S-boats – presented the biggest threat to Britain's coastal convoys after the fall of France, when bases on the Channel coast became available to them. They were up to 35m (115ft) long and displaced up to 107 tonnes (105 tons). Their three-shaft diesel engines gave them a maximum speed of anything up to 78km/h (42 knots); they had a combat radius of 1297km (700nm) at 56km/h

LEFT *A German S-boat at speed. This photograph, taken in the Mediterranean, shows one of the S-boats operating against Allied shipping supplying forces in the invasion of Sicily in 1943. Note the open door of the starboard torpedo tube.*

(30 knots) and were generally armed with two 20mm anti-aircraft guns, which could also be used for surface actions, and two 53cm (21in) torpedo tubes.

The battle begins

The S-boats' first encounter with the Royal Navy occurred on the night of 9–10 May 1940, when four craft of the 2nd S-boat Flotilla from Wilhelmshaven attacked the cruiser *Birmingham* and seven destroyers making a sortie against German minelayers in the Skagerrak. The *S31* (Lieutenant Opdenhoff) hit the destroyer HMS *Kelly* with one torpedo amidships. She was towed to Newcastle by the destroyer *Bulldog*.

Three weeks later, on 28 May, Lieutenant-Commander Rudolf Petersen, commanding the 2nd S-boat Flotilla,

called his officers together and briefed them for offensive operations in the Channel area. The evacuation of the British Expeditionary Force from France was in progress, and Petersen's orders were to enter the Channel under cover of darkness, lie in wait and strike hard at whatever British vessels were sighted, preferably those homeward bound with their cargoes of troops. Six boats were to undertake the mission, operating in two relays of three.

The first three boats slipped out of Wilhelmshaven that afternoon. In the lead was *S25*, commanded by Lieutenant Siegfried Wuppermann, an officer who was later to become one of the German Navy's small ship 'aces' in the Mediterranean. Behind him came Lieutenant Zimmermann's *S30*, followed in turn by *S34* under Lieutenant Obermaier. The outward voyage was uneventful, the S-boats entering the Channel on schedule and spreading out to take up station, engines off, to the north of the cross-Channel routes. Station was kept, from left to right, by *S30, S25* and *S34*, and after 90 minutes it was Zimmermann who made first contact with the enemy. With the aid of night glasses, he picked out a vessel and identified it as a British destroyer. Starting

ABOVE *The German motor torpedo boat* S4 *entering harbour. The larger types of S-boat were capable of carrying six or eight mines instead of spare torpedoes, and minelaying was an important part of their activities right up to the Allied invasion of Normandy in June 1944, after which they switched to more direct attacks.*

S30's engines, he closed to action stations and began his attack. At 0045 hours on 29 May, he launched four torpedoes at the target, which was the destroyer HMS *Wakeful*.

There was no time for evasive action. The first of *S30*'s torpedoes passed ahead of the destroyer but the second exploded amidships, tearing *Wakeful* in two. Within 30 seconds she was gone, leaving behind a few islands of wreckage and a handful of survivors. Over 700 men, mostly troops who had been plucked from the beaches of Dunkirk and who were crammed below decks, went to their deaths with the stricken ship. On 31 May, the French destroyer *Sirocco* was sunk by the *S23* (Lieutenant Christiansen) and *S26* (Lieutenant Fimmen), and on the next day Lieutenant Obermaier in *S34* sank the armed trawlers *Argyllshire* and *Stella Dorado*.

On 19 June, the S-boats struck their first blow against mercantile traffic in the Channel when *S19* (Lieutenant Töniges) and *S26* (Lieutenant Fimmen) sank the freighter *Roseburn* off Dungeness. On the night of 24–25 June,

S36 (Lieutenant Babbel) and *S19* sank the tanker *Albuera* and the coaster *Kingfisher* in the same area. By this time, a flotilla of five British MTBs was operating from Dover with the task of countering the S-boat threat, but it was to be some time before these craft became available in sufficient numbers to make any impression on the enemy. In any case, the S-boats were faster, bigger and better armed than the British craft, and it needed skill and judgement, which would only come with operational experience, to get the better of them.

S-boat attacks on British convoys in the English Channel intensified in July 1940, when the Luftwaffe began bombing shipping as a prelude to the start of the

BELOW: *German Schnellboote were built of wood on alloy frames, and had a round bilge hull. Maximum speed was lower than that of British MTBs, but the S-boats could sustain their maximum speed in sea states other boats could not handle. Later S-boats featured an armoured conning tower for extra protection.*

SPECIFICATIONS: *S14*

GENERAL
Ship type: Schnellboote
Entered service: 1939
Complement: 21
Fate: Scuttled May 1945

MACHINERY
Engine: Diesel
Power: Three shafts

ARMOUR
Conning tower: 51mm (2in)

ARMAMENT
Main: Two 53cm (21in) torpedo tubes
Secondary: One 20mm (0.78in) AA gun

DIMENSIONS
Length: 32.3m (106ft)
Width: 4.8m (16ft)
Height: 1.5m (4ft 9in)
Displacement: 79 tonnes (78 tons)

PERFORMANCE
Speed: 65km/h (35 knots)

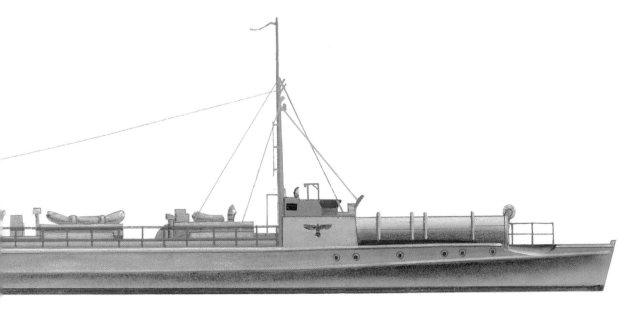

air offensive against Britain. Air attacks would be followed up by S-boat sorties against stragglers and damaged vessels, the surface attacks normally being carried out by craft of Lieutenant-Commander Birnbacher's 1st S-boat Flotilla.

The kind of destruction that could be achieved by this kind of air/sea co-operation was well illustrated on 8 August 1940, when a convoy codenamed 'Peewit', passing in daylight through the Straits of Dover, was savagely attacked by German bombers and S-boats. By the end of the day, 11 out of 21 ships, mostly colliers, had been sunk or damaged. And in another attack by the 1st S-boat Flotilla, this time on a convoy off Great Yarmouth on 4 September, four S-boats sank six freighters totalling 10,156 tonnes (9996 tons).

Countermeasures

By the winter of 1940–41 attacks by S-boats, whose numbers had now been reinforced, presented an increasingly serious threat to British coastal convoys, and in December 1940, as a countermeasure, the 6th Motor Gunboat (MGB) Flotilla was formed. It consisted of three previously converted boats, armed with four Lewis guns and one Oerlikon, and five boats originally built for the French Navy; these were armed with four Lewis guns and

four 0.303in Browning machine guns in a Boulton Paul power-operated turret. In March 1941, the 6th MGB Flotilla deployed to Felixstowe and was soon in action against the enemy, joining the existing MTB flotillas in patrolling lines from the Humber to the Hook of Holland and from Texel to the Thames. The Coastal Forces, as these light-craft flotillas were collectively known, were to be greatly expanded before the end of 1941.

By the beginning of 1941, the 1st S-Boat Flotilla had been joined by the 3rd under Lieutenant-Commander Kemnade, and on the night of 7–8 March, 12 S-boats from the two joined forces to sink seven British freighters off Cromer and Southwold. The S-boats were becoming increasingly bolder; on 18 March 1941, for example, six boats of the 1st Flotilla entered the Humber estuary, and the *S102* (Lieutenant Töniges) sank a French freighter.

In April 1941, the 3rd S-boat Flotilla was switched to the Baltic (where it was to enjoy considerable success

BELOW Schnellboote S4 *leaving harbour on a sortie. British MTBs had a difficult time against the S-boats in the early days, the latter having quiet engines and a low profile which made them difficult to detect, However, the balance shifted to the British when their more powerfully armed craft began to carry radar equipment.*

ABOVE *This photograph of Schnellboote* S18 *moving at high speed gives a good idea of the S-boats' hull structure. While serving with the 1st S-boat flotilla, Schnellboote* S18 *(Lieutenant Christian) sank the freighters* Joseph Swan *and* Nieuland *on 4 September 1940, and the* Hauxley *on 18 October of the same year.*

following the German invasion of the Soviet Union in June) and replaced by the 2nd Flotilla under Lieutenant Feldt, which began operations on 17 April, with an attack on a convoy off Great Yarmouth in which two freighters were sunk and a third damaged. The 2nd Flotilla was also redeployed to the Baltic in July, where it assumed a minelaying mission; it was joined by the 1st Flotilla in August, S-boat operations in the English Channel having been greatly reduced during the long hours of summer daylight.

Responsibility for S-boat operations in the North Sea and Channel areas now rested with the 4th Flotilla (Lieutenant-Commander Bätge), which began attacking convoys in August. Lieutenant-Commander Feldt's 2nd S-boat Flotilla also returned to the North Sea area from the Baltic in October; on 19 November it lost one of its craft,

the *S41*, which had to be abandoned after colliding with a convoy escort vessel.

Escorting the 'Channel Dash'

On 12 February 1942, S-boat Flotillas 2, 4 and 6, the latter under Lieutenant-Commander Obermaier, combined to provide part of the escort for the *Scharnhorst*, *Gneisenau* and *Prinz Eugen* during the warships' dash through the English Channel, the S-boats covering the Dutch coastal area. Minelaying subsequently accounted for much of the S-boats' activities in the spring of 1942, and on 15 March, the *S104* (Lieutenant Roeder) sank the destroyer HMS *Vortigern* during a minelaying operation in which the *S53* was also lost, having struck a mine. During this action, the *S111* was badly damaged in an enagement with British MGBs, and sank under tow.

The need to protect the Atlantic convoys bringing troops and equipment to Britain in the run-up to the Allied landings in North Africa in November 1942, meant that for some weeks the British coastal convoys were virtually stripped of escort vessels, and the S-boat commanders took full advantage of the fact. The 5th

ABOVE *Torpedoes being loaded onto a Schnellboote in northern Norway, in July 1943, prior to a sortie. S-boats were deployed to Norway to counter the attacks made on German coastal convoys by British MTBs, based in the Orkney and Shetland Islands. These MTBs were manned by crews of the Royal Norwegian Navy.*

S-boat Flotilla (Lieutenant-Commander Klug) was now operating in the Channel area, and on 2 November one of its craft, the *S112* (Lieutenant Karl Müller) sank the armed trawler *Lord Stonehaven* off Eddystone.

On 7 October, the 2nd and 4th Flotillas attacked a convoy off Cromer, sinking three freighters, one Royal

Navy tug and a motor launch, and on 14 October, Lieutenant-Commander Obermaier's 6th Flotilla torpedoed two freighters in the same area. Another freighter was sunk by Feldt's 2nd Flotilla on 9 November, and on the night of 18–19 October, the 5th Flotilla engaged a convoy off Plymouth and sank the armed trawler *Ullswater* and two coasters with torpedoes.

The first major attempt by the Germans to attack a British coastal convoy in 1943, occurred in the North Sea on the night of 24–25 January, when 16 S-boats of the 2nd, 4th and 6th Flotillas tried to attack a convoy off Lowestoft but were driven off by the destroyers *Mendip* and *Windsor*. On 3–4 February, British destroyers made a sortie from Plymouth to attack enemy shipping off Alderney, sinking two coasters, the *Hermann* and *Schleswig-Holstein*, and on the following night the Polish destroyer *Krakowiak*, which had taken part in the Alderney mission, beat off an attempted S-boat attack on a convoy near Start Point.

Protecting the convoys

As British anti-shipping aircraft became more effective in the Channel area, the S-boats moved increasingly over to the defensive, lending their firepower to German coastal convoys. The defences of the latter were now very strong; in addition to the merchant vessels themselves, which were all well-armed, the Germans used so-called Vorpostenboote (Outpost Boats), armed trawlers crammed with flak guns of all calibres, and Sperrbrecher (Barrier Breaker) ships which were former merchant vessels of up to 8128 tonnes (8000 tons).

Sweeping ahead of the convoy would be purpose-built minesweepers, the Minensuchboote, which were also heavily armed. Some of these were of World War I vintage, which Germany had been permitted to retain for coastal defence under the terms of the armistice, but others were more modern Type 35 and Type 40 vessels, armed with two 10.4cm (4.1in) guns, two 37mm and six 20mm guns. They carried a complement of between 76 and 104 and had a top speed of 33km/h (18 knots).

For close escort, there were the Raumboote or R-boats, used for coastal minesweeping, minelaying and rescue of aircrews, as well as convoy protection. Displacing 142 tonnes (140 tons) they carried a crew of 38, could make up to 39km/h (21 knots) and were armed with one 37mm and six 20mm anti-aircraft guns. Out on the flanks of the convoy there would be a screen of S-boats, and perhaps destroyers or torpedo boats. Any aircraft attacking the convoy would therefore have to contend with a storm of flak ranging in calibre from the heavy weapons (105mm and 88mm) on the Sperrbrecher, down through 40mm, 37mm, 20mm cannon and 7.92mm machine guns on the smaller escort craft and the transports themselves.

The early weeks of 1943 saw an upsurge of naval activity in the Channel area. On 27 February, the 5th S-boat Flotilla carried out a particularly audacious sortie, four craft – the *S65*, *S68*, *S81* and *S85* – penetrating into Lyme Bay and attacking a convoy that had assembled there. In a matter of minutes, they torpedoed and sank the freighter *Moldavia*, the Tank Landing Craft *LCT381* and two escort vessels, the armed trawler *Lord Hailsham* and the whaler *Harstad*.

On the night of 4–5 March 1943, *S70* struck a mine and was lost during a sortie by boats of the 2nd, 4th and 6th Flotillas into the area of Lowestoft and Great Yarmouth. The enemy craft were driven off by the destroyers *Windsor* and *Southdown* and the corvette *Sheldrake*, and the following morning the *S75* was attacked and sunk off Ijmuiden by Spitfires and Typhoons. In addition to this sortie, S-boats attempted to attack a convoy off Start Point, but this was again frustrated by accurate fire from the Polish destroyer *Krakowiak*, repeating her achievement of a month earlier. The S-boats were again active on the night of 7–8 March, attempting to attack shipping near the Sunk Lightship, but the raid was broken up by the destroyer *Mackay* and four MGBs. Two S-boats collided while taking evasive action; one of them, *S119*, was sunk by *MGB20* after her crew had been taken off by *S114*, the other craft involved in the accident.

Further successes

On the night of 13–14 April, the 5th S-boat Flotilla, led by its redoubtable commander, Lieutenant-Commander Klug, scored a resounding success off the Lizard Head in an attack on convoy PW323, comprising six merchant vessels, the Hunt class destroyers *Eskdale* and *Glaisdale*, and five armed trawlers. Four S-boats (*S90*, *S112*, *S116* and *S121*) broke through the defensive screen and S90 hit the *Eskdale* with two torpedoes, bringing her to a standstill. She was later sunk by *S65* and *S112*. Meanwhile, the 1770-tonne (1742-ton) freighter *Stanlake* was torpedoed by *S121* and finished off by the *S90* and *S82*. On 27–28 April, the destroyer HMS *Albrighton* was also damaged in a 90-minute gun battle with some S-boats off Ile de Bas.

With the advent of the light nights of summer, as in the previous year, the excursions of the S-boats into

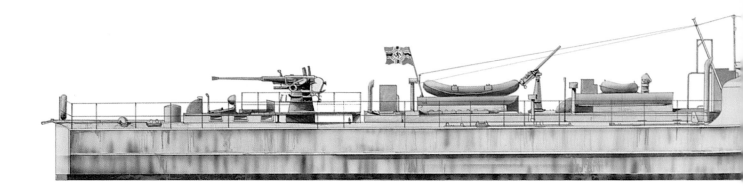

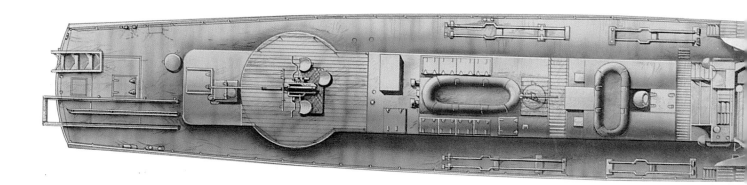

SPECIFICATIONS: *S142*

GENERAL

Ship type: Schnellboote

Entered service: 1943

Complement: 23

Fate: Sunk by RAF bombers at Le Havre
14–15 June 1944

MACHINERY

Engine: Diesel

Power: Three shafts

ARMOUR

Conning tower: 51mm (2in)

ARMAMENT

Main: Two 53cm (21in) torpedo tubes;
one 40mm (1.57in) gun

Secondary: One 20mm (0.78in) AA gun

DIMENSIONS

Length: 35m (115ft)

Width: 5m (16ft 5in)

Height: 1.9m (6ft 6in)

Displacement: 106 tonnes (105 tons)

PERFORMANCE

Speed: 78km/h (42 knots)

British waters became less frequent, and minelaying by aircraft and destroyers intensified. A major minelaying operation was undertaken during the last week in May by S-boats of the 2nd, 4th, 5th and 6th Flotillas, which laid a string of mines between Cherbourg and St Peter Port on the island of Guernsey, the Isle of Wight and Lyme Bay.

The latter objective was mined three times in June, when mines were also sown off Start Point. In all, the S-boats laid a grand total of 321 mines in the course of 77 sorties.

During this period, the main opportunities for engaging the S-boats came when the latter were

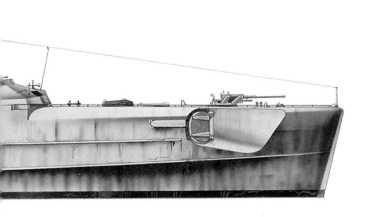

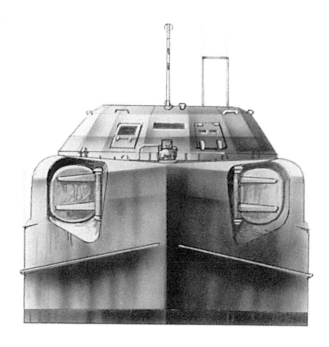

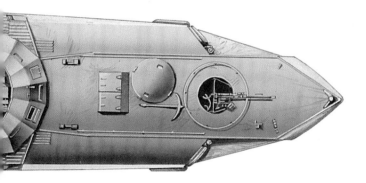

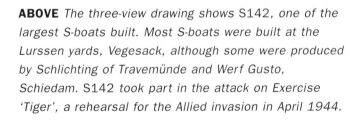

ABOVE *The three-view drawing shows S142, one of the largest S-boats built. Most S-boats were built at the Lurssen yards, Vegesack, although some were produced by Schlichting of Travemünde and Werf Gusto, Schiedam. S142* took part in the attack on Exercise 'Tiger', a rehearsal for the Allied invasion in April 1944.

detected moving from port to port. On 24–25 July 1943, for example, *S68* and *S77*, en route from Boulogne to Ostend, were attacked by British MTBs and MGBs, which sank *S77* north of Dunkirk, while on 11 August, craft of the 4th and 5th S-boat Flotillas, transferring to L'Abervach in readiness for a sortie against Plymouth Sound, were attacked by Typhoons. *S121* was sunk, *S117* badly damaged and four others slightly damaged out of the seven-boat force.

By late 1943, the Germans knew that the Allied invasion of Europe was coming; but they did not know when and where the blow would fall. In the spring of 1944, however, they launched a series of air and sea attacks on the British coast in the hope of disrupting the build-up of invasion shipping. The early months of 1944 also saw an increase in German naval activity in the Channel area, the S-boat forces having been reinforced by the 9th Flotilla. On the night of 5-6 January, seven S-boats of the 5th Flotilla (Lieutenant-Commander Karl Müller) attacked Convoy WP457 off the southwest coast of England. The boats fired a total of 23 torpedoes, swamping the escort, which was led by the destroyer HMS *Mackay*, and sank three freighters and the naval trawler *Wallasea*. The escorts proved more effective on 16-17 January, successfully driving off seven S-boats of the 5th Flotilla that tried to intercept a convoy off Lizard Head; the enemy fired eleven torpedoes, but all missed. On the last day of January, however, six boats of the 5th Flotilla attacked Convoy CW243 off Beachy Head, sinking two freighters and the naval trawler *Pine*.

A few days later, on 5 February, there was a sharp engagement between the British destroyers *Brissenden*, *Talybont*, *Tanatside* and *Wensleydale* and the German minesweepers *M156* and *M206*, escorted by the destroyer *T29*, off the coast of northern Brittany. The *M156* was badly damaged and limped into L'Abervach, where she was destroyed later by air attack.

The tide begins to turn

Some of the most intense actions during this period were fought in the North Sea, where S-boats were carrying out minelaying operations off Grimsby and Great Yarmouth. In the Channel itself, a combination of radar and rapid reaction by the escort forces were

ABOVE *The German caption to this wartime photograph states that 'The Aegean Sea area remains under strict German Navy control after the expulsion of enemy forces. Arrow-swift Schnellboote are particularly suited to this task'. In fact, much of the work in this theatre was done by Italian motor-torpedo boats.*

gradually getting the better of the S-boat forays towards the south coast. There were, nevertheless, some frenetic actions in the Straits of Dover during March, beginning on the night of the 14–15 February, when British MTBs attacked two groups of the German 36th Minesweeping Flotilla off Gravelines and sank the enemy leader, *M3630*, with a torpedo. Return fire was heavy and the British lost one boat, *MTB417*. On the following night, 10 S-boats of the 5th and 9th Flotillas (Captain von Mirbach and Captain Klug) attempted to attack Convoy WP492, escorted by the corvettes *Azalea* and *Primrose*, off Land's End. The German force was detected by air reconnaissance and other British warships in the area – the cruiser *Bellona*, the Tribal class destroyers *Ashanti* and *Tartar*, the Hunt class destroyers *Brissenden* and *Melbreak*, two minesweepers and some MTBs – diverted to intercept. Faced with this formidable weight of fire-power, the Germans had little choice but to disengage, but not before *S143* had been damaged.

The value of the British coastal radar defences in combatting the S-boat threat was again demonstrated on two nights in March, when the 5th and 9th Flotillas set out to attack shipping off the Lizard and Weymouth on the 16–17 and 20–21 February. The boats' radar detection equipment alerted the crews that they were being tracked, and the sorties were abandoned. The British coastal forces were also in action on the night of 20–21 March, when five MTBs attacked the German convoy Hecht, comprising the tanker *Rekum* escorted by the 18th Vorpostenboote Flotilla. The MTBs were beaten off, but the tanker was sunk by the Dover guns.

Exercise 'Tiger'

On the night of 27–28 April 1944, the S-boats achieved their greatest victory since 1940, and it happened more or less by accident. On that night, nine boats of the 5th and 9th Flotillas (*S100, S130, S136, S138, S140, S142, S143, S145* and *S150*) sailed from Cherbourg to attack a convoy that was reported to be off Selsey Bill. Instead, they encountered a convoy of landing craft – eight US LSTs, escorted by the corvette *Azalea*, heading from Brixham and Plymouth for Slapton Sands in South Devon where they were to take part in Exercise 'Tiger', a dress rehearsal for the American landing on Utah Beach. The convoy should also have been escorted by the destroyer HMS *Saladin*, but she had been damaged in a collision with a landing craft in Plymouth harbour and no replacement had been assigned.

The S-boats fell upon the convoy as it entered Lyme Bay, and in the torpedo attack that followed, *LST507* and *LST531* were sunk and another, *LST289*, was damaged. The loss of life was severe: 441 soldiers and 197 seamen. The attackers were pursued by the destroyers *Onslow*, *Obedient*, *Ursa*, *Piorun* and *Blyskawica*, but escaped unharmed. The incident was kept a closely guarded secret for a long time after the war, and even today there is controversy over the actual loss of life, some sources putting it as high as 749.

After the D-Day landings on 6 June 1944, the S-boat flotillas made repeated attempts to attack Allied traffic in the Channel, sinking three tank landing ships and a number of smaller craft in the first two nights and losing four S-boats to enemy action. On 14 June, the 2nd Flotilla, making for Le Havre in daylight, was attacked by two squadrons of RAF Beaufighters, which sank *S178, S189* and *S179* in that order. Worse was to come. That night, 235 Lancaster bombers of RAF Bomber Command attacked the main S-boat base at Le Havre, sinking 13 craft of the 4th, 5th and 9th Flotillas. The commander of the 5th Flotilla, Lieutenant-Commander Johanssen, was killed. Despite their losses, the S-boat commanders continued to make night sorties into the Normandy assault area throughout June, their numbers dwindling and torpedo stocks running low after 5 July, when 41 torpedoes were destroyed in an explosion at the Le Havre repair depot. By mid-July, most of the surviving S-boats were concentrated on Boulogne.

Manned torpedoes

On the night of 5–6 July the Germans brought a new weapon into action: the Neger (Negro) one-man torpedo, 26 of which were deployed against the invasion area

BELOW *While early S-boats had their torpedo tubes mounted on the deck, German Schnellboote produced later in the war had the tubes built into the hull, as shown in this photograph. Note also the additional 40mm (1.57in) cannon mounted on the bow, as well as the 20mm anti-aircraft gun at the back.*

from Villers-sur-Mer. On this occasion they sank the minesweepers *Cato* and *Magic*, and later in the month they sank the destroyer *Isis*, the minesweeper *Pylades* and disabled the Polish-manned cruiser *Dragon* so severely that she had to be scuttled as part of a Gooseberry Harbour breakwater. Neger operations ceased in mid-August, their operating unit having suffered dreadful losses. Some success was achieved during this period by Small Battle Unit Flotilla 211, which used Linsen (Lens) explosive boats to sink the destroyer *Quorn* and the anti-submarine trawler *Gairsay* on the night of 2–3 August.

The S-boats were very active during the first two weeks of August 1944, having received a quantity of the new long-range T3D Dackel torpedoes. The S-boats operated in clutches of six, three launching the Dackels and the other three acting as torpedo-carriers. Between 5 and 15 August, 77 Dackels were launched at shipping concentrations in the Seine Bay, with disappointing results; only the 5292-tonne (5208-ton) freighter *Iddesleigh* was sunk and the cruiser *Frobisher*, the repair ship *Albatros* and a minesweeper damaged.

The focus of operations now switched to the northern part of the English Channel and to the North Sea. Operating from Boulogne, the 8th S-boat Flotilla (Commander Zymalkowski), newly transferred from Rotterdam, made a number of attempted attacks on British convoys in the Dover area during the last days of August, but was beaten off by the escort, while the 8th Flotilla from Ijmuiden, under Lieutenant-Commander Alfred Müller, undertook minelaying operations off Orfordness.

A final effort

On 3–4 September, the last 13 operational S-boats in the Channel area moved to Rotterdam and Ijmuiden, *S184* being sunk en route by the Dover batteries. By the end of the year some 40 S-boats were still operating from Dutch bases against the Thames-Scheldt, east coast and Channel convoys. In the shallow waters off the east coast and in the approaches to the Scheldt, where traffic was very dense, mines laid by S-boats were the greatest threat; between January and May 1945, mines laid by the S-boats alone sank 31 merchantmen totalling 90,428 tonnes (89,000 tons). In March 1945, the British Second Army crossed the Rhine south of the Dutch frontier and swung north to cut off all land access to the German forces in Holland, which meant that the S-boats were now entirely dependent on supplies arriving by sea. Despite this, and

ABOVE *German crews leaving their S-boats after their country's surrender in early May 1945.*

despite rising losses, they went on fighting to the bitter end. Early in April, five S-boats were sunk in quick succession, and on the night of 13–14 April, during a minelaying operation by 12 boats of the 4th, 6th and 9th Flotillas, they fought their last action against British warships off the Scheldt estuary.

In the Mediterranean, S-boat operations were the prerogative of Lieutenant-Commander Kemnade's 3rd Flotilla. In December, its boats, the *S31*, *S34*, *S35*, *S55* and *S61*, carried out their first minelaying operation off Malta, and minelaying remained the Flotilla's principal occupation until June 1942, when it went into action against a Malta-bound supply convoy. In this action, Lieutenant Wuppermann in S56 damaged the cruiser *Newcastle*, and S55 (Lieutenant Horst Weber) sank the destroyer *Hasty*.

In the summer of 1943 the 3rd Flotilla redeployed to Taranto, but left on the eve of the Italian surrender. On the way through the Adriatic, they sank the Italian gun-boat *Aurora*, the Italian destroyer *Sella*, and captured the new Italian troop transport *Leopardi* with 700 troops on board. As a final flourish, arriving in Venice with their fuel tanks almost dry, the boats compelled the local commander to surrender and took over the city until reinforcements arrived.

CHAPTER 8

U-BOATS:THE WEAPON THAT NEARLY SUCCEEDED

Of all the vessels of the German Navy, the ocean-going U-boats presented the biggest threat to Allied maritime supremacy. They were defeated by a combination of hunter-killer groups, air power and Ultra, the intelligence gathered by British code-breakers. Of the 40,000 German wartime submariners, 30,000 never returned.

In August 1939, with the invasion of Poland imminent, the German Naval Staff lost no time in deploying units of the Kriegsmarine to their war stations, ready to begin an immediate offensive against Allied shipping if Britain and France declared war. On 19 August, 14 Types

LEFT: *The Type VIIC U-boat* U557 *(Lieutenant-Commander Paulshen) operated in the Mediterranean. On 16 December 1941, she was lost in a collision with the Italian torpedo boat* Orione *off Salamis, the day after sinking the British cruiser* Galatea.

VII and IX U-boats were despatched from Wilhelmshaven and Kiel and assumed waiting positions in the North Atlantic. Ten more, mostly Type IIs, were under the orders of the Commander U-boats East – Commander Schomburg – in the Baltic, but three Type VIIs (*U31*, *U32* and *U35*) were transferred to the North Sea on 2 September.

On 3 September, the U-boats struck their first blow when the *U30* (Lieutenant Lemp) torpedoed and sank the British passenger liner *Athenia* south of the Rockall Bank. About 1300 survivors were rescued by the

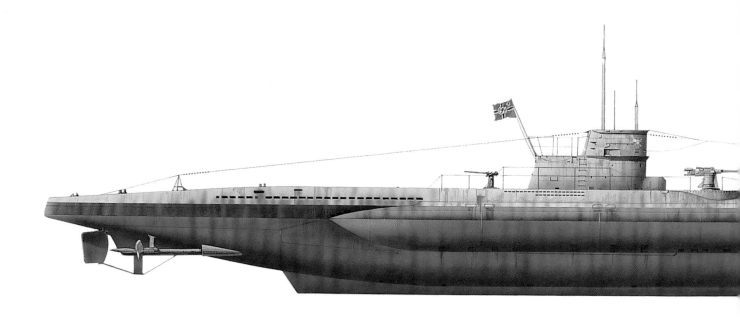

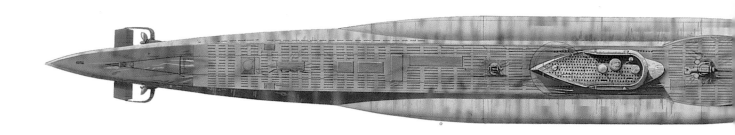

SPECIFICATIONS: *U47*

GENERAL

Ship type: Type VIIB U-boat

Entered service: 1939

Complement: 44

Fate: Sunk by depth-charge 8/3/41

MACHINERY

Engines: Diesel and electric motors

Power: Two shafts

ARMOUR

Not applicable

25mm- (1in-) strengthened hull

ARMAMENT

Main: 12 torpedoes or 14 mines

Secondary: One 8.8cm (3.5in), one 20mm (0.78in) AA gun

DIMENSIONS

Length: 66.5m (218ft)

Width: 6m (20ft)

Height: 4.7m (15ft 6in)

Displacement: 765 tonnes (753 tons)

PERFORMANCE

Speed: 31km/h (17 knots) surfaced

destroyers *Electra* and *Escort*, assisted by some foreign vessels, but 112 people lost their lives. Although the story was put out that Lemp had mistaken the liner for an armed merchant cruiser, it seems more likely that he had misconstrued his orders and believed such attacks to be permitted by the German government; whatever the truth, the British Admiralty took the sinking as evidence that unrestricted submarine warfare was in force, a belief that was to lead to the early establishment of a full convoy system for the protection of mercantile trade. In fact, the first convoy sailed on 6 September, from the Firth of Forth to the Thames Estuary, and the next day

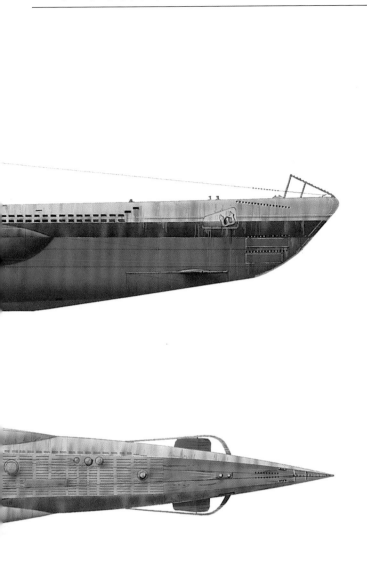

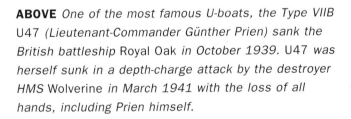

ABOVE *One of the most famous U-boats, the Type VIIB U47 (Lieutenant-Commander Günther Prien) sank the British battleship* Royal Oak *in October 1939.* U47 *was herself sunk in a depth-charge attack by the destroyer HMS* Wolverine *in March 1941 with the loss of all hands, including Prien himself.*

three escorted Atlantic convoys were also despatched, to Gibraltar, Halifax and Sierra Leone.

While the British Home Fleet continued its northern patrol – moving its main operating base from Scapa Flow to Loch Ewe on the Clyde during September for fear of air attack, the Orkneys base being very poorly defended at this time – two hunting groups, each consisting of an aircraft carrier and four destroyers, had been formed to operate against U-boats in the Western Approaches and the Channel area. Minelaying accounted for a good deal of U-boat activity, and in fact mines were responsible for the sinking of a high proportion of the 25 merchant

vessels lost in this area during September. Operations to the west of the British Isles were undertaken by 11 submarines of the 2nd U-boat Flotilla, which laid mines off Portland and in the Bristol Channel. During the same period, 11 more submarines of the 6th and 7th U-boat Flotillas, operating in the Atlantic, west of the Bay of Biscay, and off the Iberian Peninsula, sank seven merchant ships and captured two more.

A lucky escape

On 14 September, the U-boats missed their chance to deal a telling blow to the Royal Navy when the *U39* (Lieutenant-Commander Glattes) fired a salvo of torpedoes at the fleet carrier *Ark Royal*, west of the Hebrides. Luckily for the carrier, the torpedoes – a new type fitted

with magnetic pistols – detonated prematurely and the submarine was sunk by the escorting destroyers *Faulknor*, *Foxhound* and *Firedrake*, her crew being taken prisoner.

Three days later, the Royal Navy's luck ran out. On 17 September, the 22,860-tonne (22,500-ton) fleet carrier *Courageous*, with 48 aircraft, was hit by three torpedoes from the *U29* (Lieutenant-Commander Schuhart) west of the English Channel. She went down with the loss of 515 crew, and an immediate result was the withdrawal of aircraft carriers from anti-submarine operations. On 20 September, the Navy's destroyers enjoyed a revenge of sorts when the *U27* (Lieutenant-Commander Franz) was sunk off the west coast of Scotland by the *Fortuna* and *Forester*.

The arrival of the wolfpack

In October 1939, the Germans made their first attempt to conduct operations with a group of six U-boats under a single tactical commander, in this case Commander W. Hartmann. One boat, the *U40* (Lieutenant-Commander von Schmidt) was sunk by a mine in the Channel as she was outward bound, and two more, the *U42* (Lieutenant-Commander Dau) and *U45* (Lieutenant-Commander Gelhaar) were sunk by convoy escorts. The other three,

ABOVE *The U2, a Type IIA, was one of the 13 U-boats which took part in an unsuccessful operation to hunt down British submarines off Norway in March 1940. Later on in the war, she was transferred to the Baltic to continue operational duties there, but was lost in a collision on 8 April 1944.*

however, continued with the mission, each sinking one ship. Commander Hartmann's *U37* was the most successful boat of this group, sinking eight vessels (including those sunk in earlier attacks).

The biggest success in October, however, was registered by a single U-boat. On the night of 13–14 October, the German submarine *U47*, commanded by Lieutenant-Commander Günther Prien, penetrated the defences of Scapa Flow and sank the 27,940-tonne (27,500-ton) battleship *Royal Oak*, a veteran of World War I, with three torpedo hits. The attack, in which 833 lives were lost, was carried out with great coolness, skill and daring, and came as a severe shock to Britain. Prien returned home to a hero's welcome; he was to lose his own life in March 1941, when *U47* fell victim to a depth-charge attack.

Minelaying operations by U-boats and destroyers intensified during November, the submarines being active in the Straits of Dover, the Firth of Forth, off Cromarty and in the Home Fleet's new refuge of Loch Ewe. On 21 November, the cruiser *Belfast* was damaged by a mine in the Firth of Forth, and on 4 December, the battleship *Nelson* was also damaged by a mine laid by the *U31* in Loch Ewe. In the meantime the Germans had lost another U-boat; the *U35* (Lieutenant-Commander Lott), sunk by destroyers off the Orkneys. This was followed by a further loss on 4 December, when the British submarine *Salmon* (Lieutenant-Commander Bickford) attacked and sank the outward-bound *U36* (Lieutenant-Commander Frohlich) in the Heligoland Bight.

Early operations

In the seven months from September 1939 to March 1940, the U-boats sank 222 merchant ships totalling 777,040 tonnes (764,766 tons), losing 18 of their number in the process. At the start of the Norwegian campaign the Germans had 31 U-boats available for operations, divided into nine groups covering the Norwegian coastline and the North Sea across to the Shetland Islands. For their commanders, it was a frustrating time; again and again they set up impeccable attacks on British

warships and merchantmen, and time and again the torpedoes failed to explode, or malfunctioned in some other way. Five U-boats were lost during the Norwegian campaign.

The Atlantic convoys that were the U-boats' main prey in the summer of 1940 fell into several categories. First there were the convoys from Halifax, Nova Scotia, proceeding at nine or ten knots, and the slower convoys sailing at seven and a half to eight knots from Sydney, Cape Breton Island, some distance to the northwest; then there were the even slower convoys, UK-bound from Freetown, Sierra Leone, and vice versa; and also the convoys sailing to and from Gibraltar.

With U-boats and anti-shipping aircraft now established on the French Atlantic coast, all these convoys had to be re-routed. The Admiralty considered

BELOW *Designed to operate in coastal waters, the Type II U-boat was based on the Finnish-built prototype Vessiko. (see Introduction regarding other cooperation). The Type IIs were quickly ordered into production after authorisation was given in 1935, and many future U-boat aces learnt their trade in command of them.*

SPECIFICATIONS: *U3*		
GENERAL	**ARMOUR**	**DIMENSIONS**
Ship type: Type IIA coastal U-boat	Not applicable	**Length:** 40.8m (134ft)
Entered service: 1936	**25mm- (1in-) strengthened hull**	**Width:** 3.9m (13ft)
Complement: 25		**Height:** 3.8m (12ft 6in)
Fate: Broken up in 1945	**ARMAMENT**	**Displacement:** 258 tonnes (254 tons)
	Main: Six torpedoes or eight mines	
MACHINERY	**Secondary:** One 20mm (0.78in) AA gun	**PERFORMANCE**
Engines: Diesel and electric motors		**Speed:** 24km/h (13 knots) surfaced
Power: Two shafts		

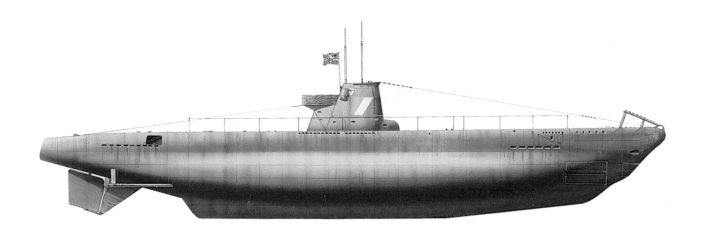

the passage southwest of Ireland to be too dangerous, and diverted the bulk of shipping to the northwest approaches and the North Channel leading to the Irish Sea. Because of the need to concentrate warships in UK waters to meet the invasion threat after the fall of France, few escort vessels were available at this time, and the enemy submarines consequently enjoyed considerable success; in June 1940 they sank 58 ships amounting to nearly 304,615 tonnes (300,000 tons), their biggest triumph so far.

Surface raiders

The U-boats were now operating in packs of four or more craft, making their attacks at night and on the surface – tactics that rendered the submarine underwater detection equipment carried by the British escort vessels useless. The Germans had used similar tactics in the 1914–18 war, and during the inter-war years had made no secret of the fact that they would use them again; the commander of the German U-boat arm, Admiral Karl Dönitz, had even described the surface night-attack method in a book published in 1939. Yet the Royal Navy's anti-submarine crews were trained only to deal with submerged submarines, and were consequently caught in

a state of unpreparedness. The result was that for a period of some months, the German submariners enjoyed a complete tactical advantage and were able to inflict heavy losses on the North Atlantic convoys – and this with never more than a paltry 15 U-boats at sea at any one time.

A game of numbers

Despite its continuing successes, however, the German submarine service was hampered by a lack of operational U-boats throughout 1940; the low priority accorded to submarine construction in the early part of the war – partly because the German Naval planners had not expected going to war before 1944 – meant that the Germans did not have enough craft coming off the slipways to replace the 31 boats lost in the first 15 months of hostilities. There was also the German training system, which required a U-boat crew to undergo nine months of training in the Baltic and carry out 66 simulated attacks before it was considered operational. The overall result was that by the end of 1940, their operational strength stood at only 22 submarines. It was fortunate for Britain that this was so, because even with the depleted U-boat resources at their disposal, the Germans came close to severing the Atlantic lifeline in the autumn of 1940. To give just one example, between 18 and 20 October, convoys SC7 and HX71 lost 31 ships between them to U-boat attacks.

Italian submarines

German submarines were not the only ones with which the Royal Navy had to contend. After some experimental forays through the Straits of Gibraltar in July and August 1940, the Italian Admiralty, the Supermarina, began to deploy submarines in considerable numbers to Bordeaux, from where they operated against the Atlantic convoys. By the end of October, 17 Italian boats were operating west of the Bay of Biscay – more submarines than the Germans had in the operational area at this particular time, although they remained under the tactical command of the German Navy.

In the summer of 1941, there was a welcome decrease in the tonnage of shipping sunk by these boats, and several factors contributed to it. From late May, continuous escort was provided for UK-bound North Atlantic convoys by groups of Canadian and British warships, something that had not previously been possible due to a lack of escort vessels; and May saw the genesis of the Atlantic 'support groups', whereby the escorts of other convoys could be diverted to strengthen the defences of one under threat. This system was first tested from 23–28 June 1941, when Convoy HX133 was attacked by 10 U-boats south of Greenland. For five days and nights a fierce battle raged between the U-boats and 13 escort vessels; five merchantmen were lost, but the escorts sank *U556* and *U651*.

The convoys in passage to and from West Africa did not yet have this system of mutual support, and it was in this theatre of the war that Italian submarines were able to exploit this lack and enjoy their limited successes.

BELOW *Type VIIA U-boat U27. This vessel was one of the submarines deployed into the North Sea before the outbreak of World War II. Her war was not to be a particularly long one. She was trapped and sunk west of the Hebrides by the destroyers HMS* Forester *and HMS* Fortune *on 22 September 1939.*

Breaking Enigma

The real key to what seemed to be a growing Allied success, however, was intelligence. On 8 May 1941, the destroyer *Bulldog*, escorting Convoy OB318, detected a German submarine prowling around the merchantmen and drove it to the surface. She was the *U110* (Lieutenant-Commander Julius Lemp). The Germans set explosive charges to deny their vessel to the enemy and abandoned ship; but the detonators failed, and a party from *Bulldog* went aboard the U-boat at no small risk to themselves and removed her code books and Enigma code machine. In the words of the official history, these captures

'*...yielded the short-range code books, which enabled GC&CS (Government Code and Cypher School) to read from May onwards the Kurzsignale, the short signals in which the U-boats transmitted their sighting reports and weather information. Captures enabled GC&CS to read all the traffic for June and July, including "officer-only" signals, currently. By the beginning of August it had finally established its mastery over the Home Waters settings (the code used by the German naval Enigma machine), a mastery which enabled it to read the whole of the traffic for the rest of the war*

SPECIFICATIONS: *U2*

GENERAL

Ship type: Type IIA coastal U-boat

Entered service: 1936

Complement: 25

Fate: Broken up in 1945

MACHINERY

Engines: Diesel and electric motors

Power: Two shafts

ARMOUR

Not applicable

25mm- (1in-) strengthened hull

ARMAMENT

Main: Six torpedoes or eight mines

Secondary: One 20mm (0.78in) AA gun

DIMENSIONS

Length: 40.8m (134ft)

Width: 3.9m (13ft)

Height: 3.8m (12ft 6in)

Displacement: 258 tonnes (254 tons)

PERFORMANCE

Speed: 24km/h (13 knots) surfaced

ABOVE *The U2 pictured earlier was designed as a short-range attack vessel for forays of limited duration, i.e. a coastal submarine. Amongst other U-boats, the U2 often fought on the surface in the early months of the war to take advantage of the fact that British tactics were designed to deal with submerged vessels only.*

except for occasional days in the second half of 1941 with little delay. The maximum delay was 72 hours and the normal delay was much less, often only a few hours.'

The Home Waters setting of the Enigma cypher, which was changed daily, carried 95 per cent of the German Navy's radio message traffic. Its yield, and that of other enemy high-grade cyphers, became known as Ultra. The breakthrough of May 1941 moved the whole war against the U-boats into a new dimension. The code-breakers and the Admiralty Submarine Tracking Room

staff now had an insight into the whole operational cycle of a U-boat, and although many months were to pass before the Tracking Room could claim to know more about the U-boats' deployment than Admiral Dönitz's own staff, the summer of 1941 was the point at which the process moved out of the realms of guesswork. It was this knowledge of U-boat movements and positions, derived from Ultra, that enabled the Admiralty to re-route convoys to avoid the U-boat packs, and it was this knowledge which enabled it to reinforce the escort of HX133, with results we have seen.

The decryption of enemy naval signals traffic was by no means new; the monitoring and decryption of enemy radio signals dated from the earliest days of August 1914, and in the anti-submarine war of 1914–18 it was perhaps the most significant contribution to British and Allied victory. During the latter half of 1941, by a very cautious estimate, the Admiralty Submarine Tracking Room, using Ultra decrypts, re-routed the convoys so cleverly around the German 'wolf-packs' that as many as 300 ships may have been saved from destruction – surely a decisive factor in the outcome of the Battle of the Atlantic.

Admiral Dönitz's U-boat offensive in the spring of 1941 had been launched in the expectation that the previously high rate of merchant ship sinkings could not only be maintained but decisively increased as more submarines were deployed. In this way the German Naval Command hoped to neutralise Britain before help arrived from the USA in significant proportions, avoiding a two-front war and leaving the German armies free to deal with the Soviet Union. In Whitehall, as the offensive got under way, the outlook was bleak. At the beginning of 1941, food stocks in Britain were dangerously low: there was enough wheat for 15 weeks; meat for only two weeks; butter for eight weeks on ration; margarine for three weeks on ration; and bacon for 27 weeks on ration. There were no longer any stocks of imported fruit. All this added up to the grim fact that, unless merchant ship sinkings could be reduced, Britain would starve before new merchant vessels could be built fast enough to maintain imports at the level needed for her survival.

Ultra

At this point, mercifully, there came the Ultra breakthrough. The intelligence it yielded came in two categories, the first and most important being that for immediate operational use. The wolf-pack tactics employed by the U-boats called for the transmission of sighting reports and homing signals between boats so that they could concentrate and attack on the surface at night in areas out of range of shore-based aircraft. Convoys were, at this time, virtually defenceless against these tactics, but their success depended on tightly centralised control by U-boat Command and the transmission of a stream of tactical orders, patrol instructions, situation reports and so on. This made them vulnerable to Ultra and to high-frequency direction finding (HF/DF). Secondly, Ultra provided huge quantities of valuable background information that included such details as the exit and approach routes from and to the U-boat bases, frequency of patrols and the rate of commissioning of new boats. It also revealed operational characteristics such as the speed, diving depths,

endurance, armament, signals and radar equipment of the various types of U-boat, and the current operational state of boats at sea.

Despite Ultra, merchant ship sinkings remained high in June 1941, partly because of difficulties in interpreting the disguised grid references for U-boat positions in the decrypts, and partly because of an increase in enemy submarine operations in West African waters, where the defences were ill-prepared and many ships were still sailing independently.

The submarines involved in these operations had to return to their bases at the end of June as they had no refuelling facilities at sea, the tankers sent out to supply them (and the *Bismarck*) all having been sunk, and when they resumed operations in this area in September they achieved comparatively little, since the convoy and escort group system was now established and the Allied ships could be routed clear of danger thanks to Ultra.

The North Atlantic saw an even more important, if not dramatic, decline in sinkings from the end of June. This was partly because steps had been taken to reduce the number of ships sailing independently, but mainly because Ultra-directed evasive routeing – in other words,

RIGHT *Admiral Karl Dönitz, Commander-in-Chief of Germany's U-boats, flanked by staff officers at his Cherbourg headquarters. Dönitz briefly became Führer after Adolf Hitler committed suicide. He was tried as a war criminal and spent 10 years in Berlin's Spandau prison.*

steering convoys clear of known U-boat patrol lines, the grid reference difficulties having been solved for the time being – could now be practised on a large scale.

The RAF fights back

By the summer of 1941, RAF Coastal Command had driven the U-boats westward, beyond the range of air patrols, which gave more scope for evasive routeing and at once brought about a sharp fall in the number of convoy attacks. Sinkings dropped from 304,815 tonnes (300,000 tons) in May and June to 101,605 tonnes (100,000 tons) in July and August. Mystified, Dönitz switched his boats back and forth in a mostly vain effort to find the elusive convoys. Although the German authorities knew that the British were obtaining valuable intelligence information, they never suspected that their naval codes had been compromised. Although they knew that the British had captured an Enigma machine, they did not know that their enemies had access to the daily settings, without which the machine was useless.

In September 1941, sinkings rose again, mainly because of renewed grid reference difficulties, but by October these had been overcome. Evasive routeing could be practised once more and sinkings again declined, despite the fact that the number of U-boats known to be at sea – now 80 – was double that at the start of the offensive. In November, sinkings dropped to 62,995 tonnes (62,000 tons), the lowest for 18 months. At this point, many boats were diverted to the Arctic and Mediterranean while the rest were mostly concentrated off Gibraltar, to which area Coastal Command's patrols were at once directed. For the time being, the offensive against the trans-Atlantic routes was virtually abandoned.

Some weeks earlier, in August, the British intelligence effort against the U-boats had been assisted by the capture of one intact. She was the *U570*, one of a group operating southwest of Iceland against Convoy HX145, which had been located by the German Signals Intelligence Service. The submarine was attacked in bad

BELOW *A German submariner making final adjustments to a G7e electric torpedo before loading it into the tube. The 'Neger' 'human torpedo' of 1944 consisted of two G7e electric torpedoes, one slung underneath the other. The upper torpedo had its warhead removed to make space for the tiny cockpit, in which the 'pilot' sat.*

SPECIFICATIONS: *U32*		
GENERAL **Ship type:** Type VII ocean-going U-boat **Entered service:** 1939 **Complement:** 44 **Fate:** Sunk by Royal Navy destroyers 30/10/40 **MACHINERY** **Engines:** Diesel and electric motors **Power:** Two shafts	**ARMOUR** **Not applicable** **25mm- (1in-) strengthened hull** **ARMAMENT** **Main:** 11 torpedoes **Secondary:** One 8.8cm (3.5in), one 20mm (0.78in) AA gun	**DIMENSIONS** **Length:** 64.5m (211ft 8in) **Width:** 5.8m (19ft) **Height:** 4.4m (14ft 5in) **Displacement:** 626 tonnes (616 tons) **PERFORMANCE** **Speed:** 29km/h (16 knots) surfaced

weather by a Lockheed Hudson of No 269 Squadron RAF, flown by Squadron Leader J. H. Thompson, and damaged; her commander, Lieutenant Hans Rahmlow, raised the flag of surrender and the Hudson continued to circle the boat until relieved by a Catalina of No 209 Squadron. The first of a succession of armed trawlers reached the scene on 27 August; the submarine's crew was taken off and she was towed to Iceland, where she was beached. Although her crew had destroyed most of the secret material on board, the capture of an intact U-boat was an important achievement. After Royal Navy service as HMS *Graph*, she was decommissioned and used in depth-charge trials, yielding important information on the effects of explosions on her pressure hull.

A breathing space

Despite the carnage that was to come, some German historians see the end of 1941 as the turning point in the Battle of the Atlantic, the 300 ships calculated as having been saved by evasive routeing not only defeating Dönitz's offensive but also providing a cushion against future heavy losses. The second half of 1941 also provided something of a breathing space in which the Allies

ABOVE *The U32 was one of the first of the Type VII ocean-going submarines and was used as the basis of all later construction. The Type VIIs were compact, cheap and simple to maintain and operate. They alone came close to starving and thus defeating Great Britain between 1941 and 1943.*

could forge ahead with the development of anti-submarine weapons and tactics, and lay the foundations for the later surge in merchant ship building which was to ensure victory.

In the autumn of 1941, Admiral Dönitz was forced to divert a number of U-boats to the Mediterranean to bolster Italy's tottering naval strength, which had taken a severe battering at the hands of the Royal Navy, and to protect the German supply lines to North Africa, under heavy attack from Malta-based aircraft and warships.

The U-boats soon made their presence felt. On 13 November 1941, the aircraft carrier *Ark Royal*, homeward bound for Gibraltar after flying off fighters to Malta, was hit near her starboard boiler room by a torpedo, one of a salvo of four fired by the German submarine *U81* (Lieutenant-Commander Guggenberger). Only one crew

member lost his life in the attack and valiant efforts were made to save the carrier, but she sank under tow only 46km (25nm) from Gibraltar.

On 25 November, the battleship *Barham,* part of Admiral Cunningham's main fleet which had put to sea from Alexandria to search for an Italian convoy, was torpedoed by the *U331* (Lieutenant von Tiesenhausen) and blew up with the loss of 861 men; there were 450 survivors.

Then, on the night of 14–15 December, the *U557* (Lieutenant-Commander Paulshen) sank the cruiser *Galatea* off Alexandria, and four days later the cruiser *Neptune* and the destroyer *Kandahar* were sunk by mines, the former with the loss of all but one of her 550 crew.

By late November 1941, the supply situation of the Axis forces in North Africa was fast becoming critical, thanks to the attacks on their convoys by the Malta-based warships, submarines and strike aircraft. In an attempt to redress matters, the Germans heavily reinforced their U-boat fleet in the Mediterranean, so that by the beginning of 1942 they had 21 boats in the theatre. These launched an offensive against the Allied convoys travelling between Egypt and the vital oil ports in the Levant, but between January and March 1942 three of them were sunk, together with five Italian submarines. The heavy losses continued with five more being sunk

ABOVE *A British merchant ship, victim of a U-boat attack, sinking in the Atlantic. Of the 5150 merchant ships (2714 British) sunk by enemy action in World War II, 2828 were sent to the bottom by submarines. The biggest annual loss was in 1942 when 1664 ships were sunk, 1160 by U-boats.*

between March and June, and five Italian boats in June and July.

Supplying the USSR

Meanwhile, in October 1941, Britain and the USA had agreed to supply the Soviet Union with 400 aircraft, 500 tanks, 200 Bren-gun carriers, 22,000 tons of rubber, 41,000 tons of aluminium, 3860 tons of machine tools and large quantities of food, medical supplies and other materials every month. It was an input that the Germans could not ignore, and on 25 December, the German Navy C-in-C, Admiral Raeder, ordered the deployment of a U-boat group code-named 'Ulan' (*U134, U454* and *U584*) to the passage south of Bear Island, between Spitzbergen and northern Norway, to lie in wait for the convoys. Their first success came on 2 January 1942, when *U134* (Lieutenant-Commander Schendel) sank the British freighter *Waziristan* of Convoy PQ7A, and on 17 January *U454* (Lieutenant-Commander Hacklander) sank the British destroyer *Matabele* which was escorting Convoy

PQ8, as well as damaging the merchant freighter *Harmatris*.

During the months that followed, the U-boats operated intensively against the Arctic convoys, with varying degrees of success. Their biggest single coup, perhaps understandably, was in June 1942, when they attacked the dispersed Convoy PQ17, sinking nine merchantmen and finishing off seven more that had been damaged earlier by air attack; but the nature of the Arctic weather and sea states often made it impossible for them to maintain contact with target vessels once the latter had been sighted, and attacks were often beaten off by escort vessels.

The Atlantic battles of 1942 began with the dispatch, early in January, of 12 Type VII-C U-boats to operate in the

BELOW *Some of the greatest U-boat successes were achieved against the Arctic convoys to Russia, despite appalling weather conditions. In this theatre, the U-boat packs operated in conjunction with German torpedo-bomber squadrons based in Norway. Matters improved for the Allies with the introduction of escort carriers.*

area of the Newfoundland Bank. Between them, from 8–12 February, they sank 21 ships.

It was the beginning of the German submariners' second 'happy time', and the operations in Canadian waters were timed to coincide with the start of Admiral Dönitz's offensive against American mercantile traffic – Operation 'Paukenschlag' ('Drumbeat') – in the western Atlantic. Only five submarines were involved in this initial deployment, yet in operations from 11 January to 7 February 1942, they sank 26 ships, all of which were sailing independently, and damaged several more. A second wave of five Type IX U-boats, operating off the eastern coast of the USA between 21 January and 6 March, sank a further 19 vessels, while off Canada another eight Type VII craft sank nine more, together with the destroyer HMS *Belmont*.

For some time, the United States Navy had been actively participating in Atlantic convoy protection work, and this activity was stepped up considerably following a meeting between Winston Churchill and President Roosevelt off Argentia, Newfoundland, on 10 August

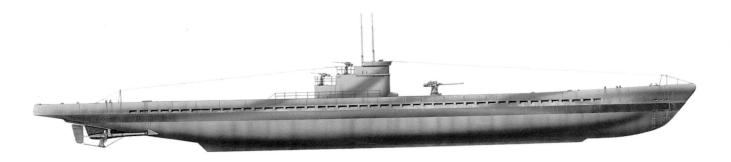

SPECIFICATIONS: *U106*

GENERAL

Ship type: Type IXB ocean-going
U-boat

Entered service: 1939

Complement: 48

Fate: Sunk by bombers 2/8/43

MACHINERY

Engines: Diesel and electric motors

Power: Two shafts

ARMOUR

Not applicable

25mm- (1in-) strengthened hull

ARMAMENT

Main: 22 torpedoes or between six and
42 mines

Secondary: One 10cm (4in) gun, one
37mm (1.5in); 20mm (0.78in) AA gun

DIMENSIONS

Length: 76.5m (251ft)

Width: 6.7m (22ft)

Height: 4.6m (15ft)

Displacement: 1068 tonnes (1051 tons)

PERFORMANCE

Speed: 33km/h (18 knots) surfaced

1941. From 17 September, the US Navy's Task Force 4 assumed responsibility for escorting the fast convoys between Newfoundland and Iceland, while the slower convoys were escorted by the Canadian Newfoundland Escort Force as far as longitude 22° West, the so-called Mid-Ocean Meeting Point, where the Royal Navy took over. The growing American participation, the increase in overall Allied escort strength, and the availability of more long-range maritime aircraft – together with the contribution of Ultra – meant that the war in the Atlantic was being won by the beginning of December 1941. In November, the U-boats sank only 13 ships, and in December the Allied shipping losses from all causes in the Atlantic amounted to just 10 vessels. Eight U-boats were destroyed in the latter month, five of them by warships escorting the Gibraltar Convoy HG76. It was in passage with this convoy that the escort carrier *Audacity* was sunk by the *U751*, but not before her Martlet fighters had shot down four FW 200 Kondor maritime reconnaissance aircraft.

The high shipping losses suffered off the eastern coast of the USA between January and April 1942 gave the British Admiralty cause for concern, for some of the vessels were British and many were tankers, which were

ABOVE *The long-range Type IX U-boats were ideal for operations in distant waters. Their hunting ground was the Indian Ocean, where they used Japanese bases for replenishment. They had a surface endurance of 16,100km (8700nm) at 12 knots. All Type IX U-boats ceased operations with the surrender of Germany in early May 1945.*

in short supply; and it must be said that the German successes during this period were attributable not so much to the skill and daring of their submariners, although they possessed both qualities in plenty, but to mistakes in strategy made by the Americans. They failed to institute an immediate convoy system, despite British urging for them to do so, and as a result targets sailing independently, close to a coastline that was still often lit at night, were easy to sight, track and sink.

The Americans advanced a number of reasons for not implementing a convoy system on British lines – lack of sufficient escorts, the danger of concentrating targets and so on – but there was a human factor involved as well. Admiral Ernest King, the Commander-in-Chief United States Fleet, believed that offensive tactics by patrol groups would produce better results. Apart from that, he was by no means an admirer of the British, and the idea of adopting a convoy system and naval control of shipping on the British pattern ran contrary to his nature. It was not until May 1942 that the Americans established a system of convoy on their east coast routes, and the result was immediately apparent: the U-boats were forced to switch their main area of operations to the Gulf of Mexico and the Caribbean, and it was only there that they continued to register successes for the next three months or so, until the convoy system was extended to cover these sectors too.

It was at about this time that anti-submarine aircraft began to make their mark. During their 'happy time' off the US coast the U-boat crews had had practically nothing to fear from shore-based aircraft, as no experienced American ASW squadrons were available, and when Dönitz switched the weight of the U-boat offensive back to the North Atlantic convoy route, in July 1942, most of the submarine operations took place in the 'air gap' outside the range of aircraft operating from Newfoundland, Iceland and Northern Ireland. To add to the Allies' problems, in February 1942 the Germans had introduced a new and more complex form of Enigma cypher solely for use with U-boats at sea, except for those in the Arctic and Mediterranean, and had tightened up security all round. Called 'Triton' by the Germans, this new cypher defeated

the experts for 10 months and deprived the Allies (the Americans having been admitted to the Ultra secret well before Pearl Harbor) of their special knowledge of U-boat operations.

The one area in which Ultra was still useful was the Bay of Biscay, for the specialists were able to decrypt the Hydra cypher used by patrol vessels escorting the U-boats in and out. It was the custom of the submarines to traverse the bay submerged by day and to recharge their batteries on the surface at night, when there was minimal risk from the patrolling aircraft of Coastal Command's No 19 Group, but on 6 July the cover of darkness was suddenly stripped away when the *U502* was attacked and sunk by a Wellington of No 172 Squadron, equipped with a searchlight. Following more 'Leigh Light' attacks the German U-boat Command changed its tactics; submarines were now directed to pass through the Bay at night submerged and surface to recharge their batteries in daylight, when aircraft could be detected visually in time for the boat to dive.

The Germans had good reason to be satisfied with the results obtained by their U-boats in the first half of 1942; in all waters they had sunk 585 merchantmen totalling more than 3,048,150 tonnes (3,000,000 tons). They had commissioned over 100 new boats and lost 21, only six of which had been sunk in the western Atlantic.

The 'air gap'

From July to December 1942, many convoys were attacked in the 'air gap'. The situation might have been alleviated by the provision of more very long range (VLR) aircraft to Coastal Command (at this time, No 120 Squadron, operating from Northern Ireland with detachments to Iceland, was the Command's only VLR unit, and it had only five Liberators). For some inexplicable reason, the 32 Liberators allocated to Coastal Command between July and September 1942 were not modified to VLR standard, but instead were given to Nos 59 and 224 Squadrons, in southwest England, to strengthen the Bay patrols.

As for ASV (Air to Surface Vessel) radar, the Mk II set had been used by Coastal Command since the end of 1940, but it had its drawbacks. Its range was limited to

LEFT *U-boats operating in northern areas of the Baltic had to contend with icy conditions for much of the year. Their presence was instrumental in preventing the breakout of the Soviet fleet from its naval base at Kronstadt. They also operated in the Black Sea.*

about 22km (12nm) on an operational target – a fully surfaced submarine – and then only when the boat was lying beam-on to an aircraft flying at 610m (2000ft) or more. The main disadvantages of the equipment were a strong back echo, excessive sea returns, bulky aerials and a rather high optimum search height. Nevertheless, ASV Mk II was a proven success, and the number of U-boat sightings initially quadrupled after aircraft fitted with this equipment began operating at night to catch the enemy submarines on the surface.

In the summer of 1941, the first ASV Mk II sets were supplied to the Americans, who were not yet at war, and these were installed in one PBY-5 Catalina each of Navy Patrol Squadrons VP-71, VP-72 and VP-73, and in two PBM-1 Mariners of VP-74. Additional aircraft were equipped in September. The squadrons all belonged to Patrol Wing 7, which became the first unit in the US Navy to be supplied with radar-equipped aircraft. The Catalinas and Mariners operated from Norfolk, Virginia, Quonset Point and advanced bases in Newfoundland and Iceland during the last months of America's 'neutrality patrol' prior to the attack on Pearl Harbor. Thereafter, Patrol Wing 7 joined the war against the U-boat.

In the spring of 1942, British ASV operations suffered a setback when a Lockheed Hudson fitted with ASV Mk II

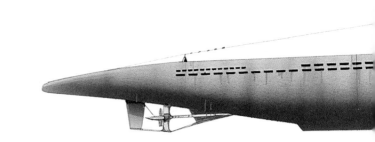

ABOVE *Planned at time when the idea of a large cruiser submarine was in fashion, four Type XI craft were projected but never built. They were mainly intended for surface actions, and even had provision for carrying their own spotter aircraft.*

BELOW *The crew of the U558 falls in to welcome the U372 as she returns to base after an Atlantic sortie. A Type VIIC, U372 was sunk in the Mediterranean off Jaffa by RN destroyers on 4 August 1942; U558 was bombed and sunk in the Bay of Biscay on 20 July 1943.*

SPECIFICATIONS: *U112*

GENERAL

Ship type: Type XI cruiser submarine

Entered service: Projected only

Complement: 112

Fate: Project abandoned

MACHINERY

Engines: Diesel and electric motors

Power: Two shafts

ARMOUR

Not known

ARMAMENT

Main: Four 12.7cm (5in) guns; 12 torpedoes

Secondary: Two 37mm (1.5in), two 20mm (0.78in) AA guns; one aircraft

DIMENSIONS

Length: 115m (377ft)

Width: 9.5m (31ft)

Height: 6m (20ft)

Displacement: 3190 tonnes (3140 tons)

PERFORMANCE

Speed: 43km/h (23 knots) surfaced

fell into enemy hands in Tunisia. Within a matter of months the Germans had produced a search receiver for installation in their U-boat fleet. Code-named 'Metox', the receiver gave warning of the approach of an aircraft using ASV Mk II from about 56km (30nm), which gave the U-boat ample time to evade. As a consequence, the number of U-boat sightings dropped dramatically in the latter half of 1942 as the tactical initiative was restored to the submarines.

One measure that did give the Allies a considerable advantage in the Atlantic battles of 1942, however, was the large-scale introduction of shipborne HF/DF (High Frequency/Direction Finding) equipment, known as 'Huff-Duff' to those who used it. The wolfpack tactics employed by the U-boats required them to make radio reports to their shore stations when they made or lost contact with a convoy, and a single HF/DF ship could provide reliable detection of a U-boat making a transmission on the frequency the ship was guarding when the latter was within 'ground wave' range, 28-56km (15-30nm). Each HF/DF report enabled the escort commander to send an escorting aircraft if he had one, or anti-submarine

ships to search for and attack the U-boat. The submarines needed their surface speed to keep up with or overtake a convoy, and even if the searching escorts failed to find and attack the U-boat, they could probably force it to submerge until the convoy was out of sight. By the end of January 1942, 25 escorts had been fitted with HF/DF, and the number increased steadily throughout the year. Next to centimetric radar, HF/DF was probably the most important element in winning the Battle of the Atlantic. In combination with radar, it eventually made submarine attacks on convoys too hazardous to be attempted.

In 1942, though, despite the growing number of Allied surface and air escorts, and despite the introduction of new equipment, merchant shipping losses mounted to unprecedented levels, and in November they reached an all-time record of 711,235 tonnes (700,000 tons). The Germans were now suffering severe reverses in the Soviet Union and North Africa, and the Atlantic seemed the one area in which they could inflict terrible damage on the Allies. With Allied shipping under immense strain the outlook was bleak, and the optimism of 12 months earlier had vanished. When the figures for

1942 were added up, they reached the appalling total of 1664 merchantmen – 8,128,400 tonnes (8,000,000 tons) – lost on the high seas. Unless this rate of loss could be reduced there seemed no prospect that the construction of new merchant tonnage could outstrip sinkings, and the gloomy economic news was that Britain's imports had fallen to two-thirds of the 1939 total.

In December 1942, in desperation, the Admiralty turned to the code-breakers for help. It was not slow in coming, for in that very month, by an astonishing coincidence, documents from a U-boat sunk off Port Said enabled the experts at last to break into the Triton cypher. The decrypts revealed that Admiral Dönitz now had over 100 U-boats deployed; 50 were in the Atlantic, and 37 of them were operating in the 'air gap' to the south of Greenland.

The timely breaking of Triton, together with terrible weather conditions – which hampered the U-boats as much as the convoys in the early weeks of 1943 – meant that the Admiralty could once again adopt evasive routeing, which undoubtedly saved many ships in January. As an added bonus, the Germans' own cypher-breaking service, the xB-Dienst, temporarily lost its ability to read the British Convoy Cypher, which robbed the U-boats of vital intelligence. As a result, sinkings dropped dramatically

during this period, although from 3-12 January the U-boats scored a notable success by sinking seven out of nine tankers in Convoy TM1, running from Trinidad to Gibraltar.

Then, in February, the xB-Dienst restored its ability to read the Convoy Cypher, and the U-boats attacked in groups of unprecedented size. Between 2 and 9 February, 20 boats of the Pfeil (Arrow) and Haudegen (Broadsword) groups fell on the slow Convoy SC118 between Newfoundland and Iceland and sank 13 of its 63 ships. Later in the month, 16 U-boats were directed to attack the outward Convoy ON166, sinking 14 of its 40 ships, while other convoys were attacked in the Central Atlantic by U-boats replenishing from 'Milchkuh' supply submarines near the Azores.

Allied losses for February amounted to 63 ships totalling 365,778 tonnes (360,000 tons), and worse was to come. In March, the cypher experts lost their grip on

BELOW *Designed for an ultimate submerged speed of 46km/h (25 knots) with the introduction of a Walter turbine engine, a dozen examples of the Type XVIIG U-boat were planned, but the project was cancelled. Apart from slight modifications, the boat was similar to the XVIIB, built for operations in coastal waters.*

SPECIFICATIONS: *U1081*

GENERAL
Ship type: Type XVIIG U-boat
Entered service: Not applicable
Complement: 19
Fate: Cancelled

MACHINERY
Engine: Diesel
Power: Single-shaft Walter geared turbine

ARMOUR
Not applicable

ARMAMENT
Main: Four torpedoes

DIMENSIONS
Length: 40.5m (129ft 6in)
Width: 3.3m (11ft)
Height: 4.3m (14ft)
Displacement: 319 tonnes (314 tons)

PERFORMANCE
Speed: 43km/h (23 knots) surfaced

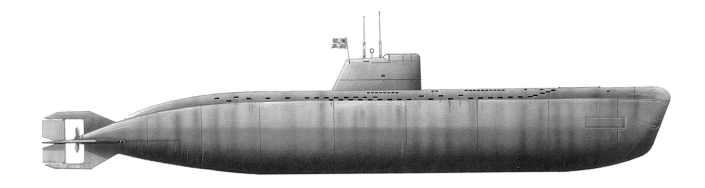

ABOVE *A Type VIIC U-boat leaving harbour, its crew dressed on deck. Because of reports transmitted to Britain by the French resistance, it was very difficult for a U-boat to leave a base on the French Atlantic coast without British air and naval forces waiting to trap it as it made the dangerous crossing of the Bay of Biscay.*

Triton for a fortnight, with the result that this month became the worst ever for convoy sinkings.

It began with an attack on the slow Convoy SC121, which lost 13 ships between 7 and 11 March. Then, from the 16-20 March, Convoys SC122 (60 ships) and HX229 (40 ships), both outbound from New York, were attacked by 40 U-boats. The HX convoy lost 21 merchantmen totalling 143,263 tonnes (141,000 tons); SC122 lost nine. In all theatres of war, in that terrible month, the U-boats sank 108 ships totalling 637,063 tonnes (627,000 tons). Losses were so severe, in fact, that the naval staff later recorded that the enemy had come 'very near to disrupting communications between the New World and the Old.' Compounding the tragedy was the fact that the two convoys from New York had been re-routed from the northern to the southern route to avoid the Raubgraf U-boat group, which was shadowing another convoy, ON170.

But the tide was about to turn. In March, as the Atlantic battles raged, representatives of the British, American and Canadian navies met in an 'Atlantic Convoy Conference' in Washington. It was agreed that the US Navy should assume responsibility for the tanker convoys running between Britain and the West Indies, leaving the North Atlantic entirely to the British and Canadians. The Royal Canadian Navy, directed by a new Northwest Atlantic Command HQ at Halifax, would be entirely responsible for the North Atlantic convoys as far as 47° West, where the Royal Navy would take over. March also saw the formation of the first Support Groups, which would provide rapid reinforcement for convoys under threat; two of the first five were composed of destroyers drawn from the Home Fleet, two of escort vessels from the Western Approaches Command, all with highly experienced crews, and the fifth was formed around the escort carrier HMS *Biter*.

In April 1943, the cryptoanalysts once again made a partial inroad into the Triton cypher, with the result that evasive routeing could be re-established. It was not always a success, being often frustrated by xB-Dienst countermeasures. The real Allied successes at this juncture came with new operational capabilities. By the end of March, Coastal Command's slowly growing force of VLR Liberators and Boeing Fortresses (the latter serving with Nos 206 and 220 Squadrons), together with aircraft from HMS *Biter*, were closing the Greenland gap and forcing U-boat shadowers to submerge. Improved

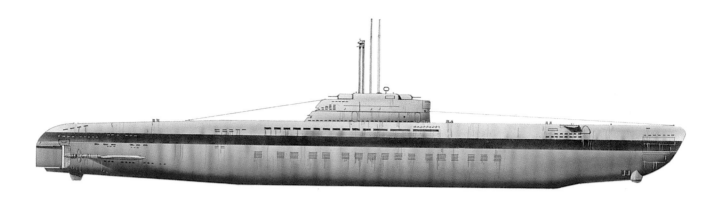

SPECIFICATIONS: *U2511*

GENERAL

Ship type: Type XXI ocean-going U-boat
Entered service: 1945
Complement: 57
Fate: Surrendered May 1945

MACHINERY

Engines: Diesel/silent electric motors
Power: Single shaft

ARMOUR

Not applicable

ARMAMENT

Main: 23 torpedoes or 12 plus 12 mines
Secondary: Four 30mm (1.17in) AA guns

DIMENSIONS

Length: 76.5m (251ft)
Width: 7m (21ft 6in)
Height: 6m (20ft)
Displacement: 1638 tonnes (1612 tons)

PERFORMANCE

Speed: 29km/h (16 knots) surfaced

anti-submarine tactics and weapons began to make themselves felt. Shipborne HF/DF maximised its exploitation of U-boat transmissions, often helping convoys to steer clear of danger and assisting air and surface escorts to seek out and kill the enemy. Above all, centimetric radar, now installed in surface escorts and (as ASV Mk III) in aircraft, was turning them into deadly U-boat killers. The German Navy sought frantically for countermeasures, but it was not until September 1943 that the Germans realised that only 10cm ASV radar was being used. Their response was to modify the non-directional S-band Naxos night-fighter receiver, which the Luftwaffe used to home on transmissions from H2S radar sets carried by British bombers, for U-boat use. Operating between 8 and 12cm, Naxos was found to be capable of detecting ASV Mk III transmissions to a range of about 18.5km (10nm).

That, however, was in the future, and meanwhile, in the three months to the end of May 1943, the Allies sank 56 U-boats – 41 in May alone – compared with the 51 that left port, so that for the first time there was a net decrease in their operational number. The number lost in the period January–May was 96, of which 52 were sunk by aircraft. Signs of flagging morale now became apparent in the Triton decrypts, together with references to the

ABOVE *The Type XXI U-boat was an ocean-going submarine capable of fully submerged operations using Schnorchel and conventional diesel/electric propulsion. The hull was streamlined, of all-welded construction and, in order to speed production, was prefabricated in eight sections.*

U-boat crews' growing fear of air attack and the speed with which the escorts and Support Groups reacted to sightings. By 19 April, Dönitz was conceding that Allied reaction – in particular maritime air – was frustrating the U-boat 'pack attack' concept, and on 25 May he withdrew his submarines to the Central Atlantic, outside the radius of Allied land-based air cover and where convoys were less well defended.

In this area the U-boats had already scored considerable success in April; on 30 April a single submarine, the Type IX *U515* (Lieutenant-Commander Henke), made three attacks on Convoy TS37 between Takoradi and Sierra Leone and sank seven of its 18 ships, totalling 43,950 tonnes (43,255 tons). During this series of battles, each side became aware that the other was learning of the movements and whereabouts of the opposing forces; the Allies, now convinced that the Convoy Cypher had been compromised, immediately brought a new one into force, and from June 1943 onwards, the Germans were denied virtually all intelligence of Allied shipping movements. Adding to the Germans' problems was an order from Dönitz insisting that U-boats traverse the Bay of Biscay on the surface by day in the erroneous belief that they would be able to shoot it out with Allied aircraft. The maritime crews took every advantage of the order, and in the 94 days that it remained in force, from 1 May to 2 August 1943, they sank 28 U-boats in the Bay. But the success was not without its cost; 57 aircraft failed to return.

From the end of July 1943, the British and American cryptoanalysts were able to break the Triton cypher until almost the end of the war, with only very rare delays. Its recovery was ably demonstrated when, with its assistance, American escort carriers and Coastal Command between them sank almost the entire fleet of Milchkuh supply submarines (only 10 were ever built). This reduced the U-boat campaign in distant waters to negligible proportions, and greatly diminished the effectiveness of the boats operating in the Central Atlantic.

Hunting the U-boats

The success of the Allied achievement in the summer of 1943 may be judged by the fact that not one North Atlantic convoy was attacked in June, and in the Central Atlantic U-boats were suffering from the attentions of US carrier aircraft. The lack of activity now enabled the Admiralty to move from defence to attack, and on 20 June, the 2nd Escort Group under Captain F.J. Walker was ordered into the Bay to hunt U-boats in conjunction with aircraft. The Milchkuh tanker submarine *U119* was rammed and sunk by the sloop *Starling*, while the *U449* was depth-charged and sunk by *Wild Goose*, *Woodpecker*, *Kite* and *Wren*. Other escort and support groups also participated in these operations, relieving one another at intervals of five to eight days and sinking two more U-boats, to bring the June total (in the Bay) to a somewhat disappointing four. Only 17 were sunk in all waters during the month.

In September 1943, Admiral Dönitz ordered group operations against the Atlantic convoys to resume, the U-boats now being equipped with search receiver equipment, eight 20mm anti-aircraft guns and a new acoustic homing torpedo, the T5 *Zaunkönig* (Wren). Twenty submarines passed through the Bay of Biscay to operate against Convoys ON202 and ONS18 on the eastern side of the North Atlantic. The Admiralty was advised of the movement by Ultra and a Liberator of No 10 Squadron

RCAF sank the *U341* in the southern part of the patrol line on 19 September. However, because of grid reference problems, the position of the first attack wave was miscalculated by 185km (100nm), and the U-boats were able to achieve a measure of surprise. In a five-day battle, they sank three escorts and six merchantmen, losing three of their own number, but the U-boats were frustrated by the rapid reaction of Support Group B3 under Commander M.J. Evans, with 18 destroyers, corvettes and frigates, and by the VLR Liberators which flew constantly over the convoys when the weather permitted. German claims to have sunk 12 escorts with 24 T5 firings resulted in the effectiveness of the new torpedo being greatly overestimated; in fact, many of the torpedoes failed to explode or detonated in the ships' wash.

Other operations against the Atlantic convoys culminated in a disaster for the U-boats. In an attack on Convoys ON206 and ONS20 between 15 and 18 October, the submarines sank only one merchantman and lost six of their number, three to aircraft. In all, Dönitz lost 25 U-boats in the Atlantic during September and October 1943, and they achieved nothing more than the sinking of nine merchant ships out of the 2468 convoyed across the ocean.

More escort carriers were now available for operations in the Atlantic. HMS *Tracker*, for example, was now working in conjunction with Captain F.J. Walker's 2nd Escort Group, and it was Walker who devised simple but effective tactics to make the U-boats' lives even more difficult. Once search aircraft from the carrier had made contact with a submarine and directed Walker's ships on to it, he would position a 'directing ship' astern of the enemy to maintain ASDIC contact. Meanwhile, two other escorts, not using their ASDIC, would creep up on either side of the submarine and release depth-charge patterns on the command of the director vessel, giving the U-boat no time to take avoiding action.

The end of the wolfpacks

Such vigorous action by air and surface forces, together with evasive routeing, compelled Dönitz to abandon his wolfpack tactics in November 1943, and to withdraw all but a few boats from the North Atlantic, where they continued for months to hunt for convoys with negligible success. The main U-boat forces were sent to operate against the Gibraltar convoys, where they had the advantage of air support, and during the ensuing months, many battles were fought in Iberian waters and the southwestern approaches. But here, too, frustrated by Ultra-directed

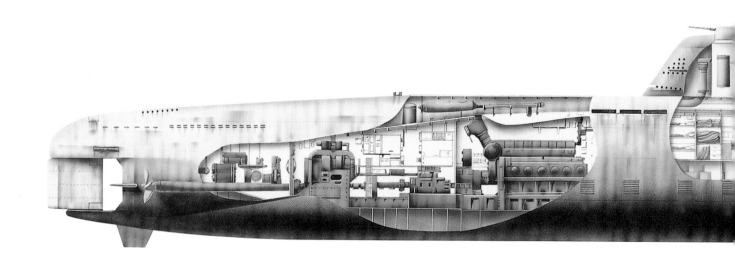

ABOVE *A cut-away diagram of the Type XXI U-boat. Note that there is no deck gun fixed to the hull. The chin sonar and sonar masts were the prominent feature of this design. For specifications see page 152.*

air patrols, support groups and evasive routeing, they achieved little and suffered heavy losses. From 13-21 November, for example, some 30 U-boats with strong maritime air support, operated against the combined Convoys MKS30 and SL140 on the Gibraltar route, but determined attacks by air and surface escorts fended the submarines off and the only two merchantmen (out of 66) lost were sunk by Hs 293 glider bombs launched by Heinkel He 177s. Three U-boats were sunk.

From January–March 1944 only three merchant ships were sunk out of 3360 convoyed, and in the whole of 1944, only 36 were sunk. Maritime air was the major factor in this, and by 1944, as Ultra revealed, the U-boats were reporting that air attacks in the Central Atlantic were even more serious than those in the Bay of Biscay. Such was the background to the successful transport of US forces to Britain, making it possible to launch the Normandy invasion on time.

In the Arctic, too, the remaining U-boats suffered grievous losses in the early months of 1944. In March 1944, for example, Convoy JW58 – with 49 ships, the largest convoy so far to sail on the Arctic route – accompanied by the cruiser *Diadem*, the escort carriers *Tracker* and *Activity*, 20 destroyers, five sloops and five corvettes (an escort that included Captain Walker's 2nd Support Group), was a tempting target for the German submarines. On 29 March, the 2nd Support Group scored

an early success when it sank the *U961*, en route to the Atlantic, and during the next three days Martlet fighters from the escort carriers shot down three FW200, two Ju88 and one Bv138 reconnaissance aircraft. Three U-boat groups, Thor, Blitz and Hammer, with 12 boats between them and assisted by five more bound for the Atlantic, made repeated attacks on the convoy, but without success; the *U355* was sunk by the destroyer *Beagle*, following a rocket attack by one of *Tracker*'s Avengers, the *U360* was destroyed by the *Keppel*, and the *U288* was sunk by aircraft from the two carriers, all between 1 and 3 April. The convoy, meanwhile, made steady progress.

As the date for the Allied invasion of Normandy approached, one major concern of the Allied Naval Command was to prevent interference by U-boats, in particular those equipped with the new Schnorchel device which enabled them to stay submerged, without the need to surface to recharge their systems. In fact, when the invasion (codenamed Operation 'Overlord') began, there was such a large concentration of Allied air squadrons west of the Channel entrance, making radar searches by day and night, that it was impossible for

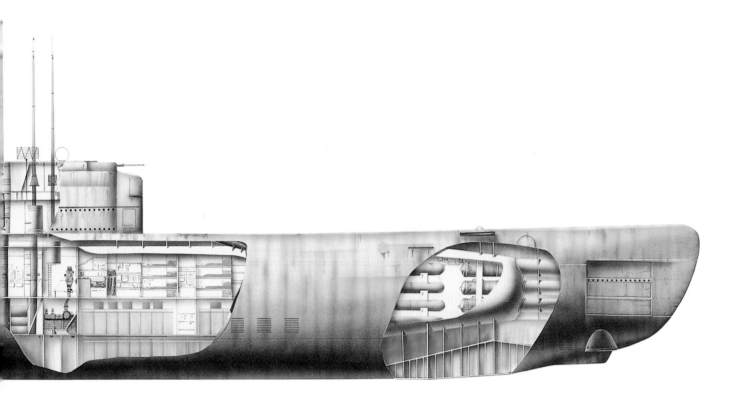

U-boats without Schnorchel to come anywhere near the invasion area. All those that tried were heavily attacked by aircraft and either sunk or damaged so that they had to return to base or were recalled by the Commander U-boats. The Schnorchel boats were able to evade the air attacks, but they then had to face very strong naval anti-submarine groups concentrated in the Channel entrance, and only very few were able, after a fortnight or so, to enter the 'funnel', where they achieved minimal success.

Ten Support Groups of destroyers, sloops and frigates formed a screen at either end of the Channel; six covered the Western Approaches and the Bay of Biscay, supported by the escort carriers *Activity*, *Tracker* and *Vindex*.

For some time, the Germans had been holding anti-invasion U-boats at readiness in French and Norwegian harbours, and when the invasion began the Biscay group was ordered to proceed to the scene of the landings. On 6 June, 17 U-boats put to sea from Brest, 14 from St Nazaire, four from La Pallice and one from Lorient. They were soon in trouble; the next day, aircraft of No 19 Group Coastal Command sank the *U955* and *U970* in the Bay of Biscay, and four of the Brest boats, U963, U989, *U256* and *U415* were all damaged and forced to return to base. On 8 June, a Liberator of No 224 Squadron sank the *U629* and *U373* in rapid succession, and on 9 June the *U740* was also destroyed. Only nine U-boats of the Biscay group were Schnorchel-equipped, and eight of

these attempted to infiltrate the Channel area from 7 June. Between that date and 11 June, three made abortive torpedo attacks, and *U821* was destroyed by an aircraft. It was not until 15 June that they enjoyed some success, the *U621* sinking the tank landing ship *LST280*, the *U767* the frigate *Mourne*, and the *U764* the frigate *Blackwood*; the latter was taken in tow, but was a total loss. On 18 June, *U767* was sunk by destroyers of the 14th Support Group, and the *U441* by a Wellington of No 304 (Polish) Squadron.

A second group of Schnorchel-equipped submarines penetrated the invasion area during the second half of June, and these suffered an early loss when *U971* was sunk in the western part of the Channel by the destroyers *Haida* and *Eskimo* on the night of 22–23 June. Two nights later, the destroyers *Affleck* and *Balfour* sank the *U1191*, while the *U269* was destroyed by the *Bickerton*; the destroyer *Goodson* was torpedoed and damaged by the *U984*. On 27-29 June, *U988* torpedoed the corvette *Pink*, which was a total loss, and sank two ships of 9595 tonnes (9444 tons) before she was sent to the bottom by the 3rd Support Group. The biggest German success came that same day, 29 June, when the *U984* attacked Convoy EMC17 and torpedoed four ships totalling 29,252 tonnes (28,790 tons), three of which were sunk and the fourth beached. This attack showed what a Schnorchel boat could achieve under favourable

circumstances, and it must be said that the U-boat operations in June 1944 had been dogged by technical failures; often, their torpedoes had detonated prematurely, or their motors had failed to work properly.

On 26 June, after a heavy bombardment by naval forces, Cherbourg fell to the Americans, and another vital port was lost to the enemy. Ultra now began to detect a steady movement of enemy submarines away from France to Norway; this transfer was accomplished with surprisingly few losses, because the U-boats could travel submerged and search aircraft were unable to locate the Schnorchel-heads in the sea clutter when they were raised above the surface at night for re-charging the batteries.

During the winter of 1944–45, the Schnorchel U-boats launched their final offensive against Allied shipping, but such was the weight of air and sea power ranged against them that their freedom of movement was severely restricted. Early in 1945, the British anti-submarine forces swamped the sea areas around the British Isles, inflicting such heavy losses on the U-boats that they were forced out of the coastal waters. Between 15 November 1944 and 27 January 1945, the U-boats sank 31 ships, but they also lost 12 of their number. At the end of January, the new Type XXIII boats became operational,

ABOVE *The Allies began to win the war against the U-boats with the introduction of very long-range patrol aircraft such as the Consolidated Liberator. The code letters on this aircraft denote that it belonged to No 220 Squadron, RAF Coastal Command, which was based in Northern Ireland and then later in the Azores.*

and in the following five-week period they sank 16 ships and damaged several others; but 10 more U-boats fell victim to the anti-submarine forces.

The Type XXIII was one of two types of submarine on which Admiral Dönitz had pinned great hopes. Designed for operations in coastal waters, it displaced 260 tonnes (256 tons), was 34m (112ft) in length and carried a crew of 14. The point about the Type XXIII was that it was a diesel-electric boat, and therefore very quiet. A much larger variant was the Type XXI. Displacing 1678 tonnes (1652 tons) submerged, it was an ocean-going craft capable of fully submerged operations using Schnorchel and conventional diesel-electric drive. Its submerged speed was 29km/h (16 knots) and it was armed with 23 torpedoes. For ease and speed of building, it was constructed in prefabricated sections. Admiral Dönitz planned to renew operations against the Allied convoys with the Type XXI late in 1944, but construction was frustrated by the Allied bombing campaign and it never became operational.

The U-boats fought on to the end, and on 5 April they suddenly returned to British coastal waters. In a desperate, last-ditch offensive lasting a month, they sank eight ships, but 15 submarines were destroyed. Yet they nearly had the last word. On 7 May 1945, the day before Germany capitulated, the *U2336* (Lieutenant Klusmeyer) sank the freighter *Avondale Park* in the Firth of Forth. That afternoon though, a Catalina of No 210 Squadron sank the *U320* (Lieutenant Emmrich) off Bergen. It was the last U-boat to be destroyed in World War II.

From 1943, U-boats also operated in the Indian Ocean. In February 1943, after replenishing from the 'Milchkuh' (Type XIV) tanker and supply submarine *U459* in the South Atlantic, the Seehund (Seadog) U-boat

BELOW *Caught on the surface in passage across the Bay of Biscay, a Type VIIC U-boat is attacked and bombed by a Liberator. In 1943, U-boat commanders were ordered to make the Biscay crossing on the surface and shoot it out with aircraft. U-boat losses were heavy, but the patrol aircraft also suffered.*

group, comprising the *U160*, *U182*, *U506*, *U509* and *U516* began operations in the Indian Ocean off South Africa, and in two and a half months, they sank 20 ships before returning to their French bases. The *U182* was sunk en route by the US destroyer *Mackenzie*.

A second wave of eight U-boats (*U177*, *U178*, *U180*, *U181*, *U195*, *U196*, *U197* and *U198*) arrived in the Indian Ocean in April; replenishing from the tanker *Charlotte Schliemann*, they sank 42 ships off Mauritius, South Africa and East Africa by the end of August. *U197* was sunk by Catalina aircraft on 20 August; the remainder, with the exception of *U178* – which went to the Japanese naval base at Penang, Malaya – returned to Bordeaux.

September 1943 saw the 'Monsun' U-boat group (*U168*, *U183*, *U188*, *U532* and *U533*) operating off the west coast of India, in the Gulf of Oman and the Gulf of Aden. By the end of October, they had sunk six freighters and a number of sailing vessels. The total would have been higher had it not been for continual torpedo failures. The *U533* was bombed and sunk in the Gulf of Oman on 16 October. The surviving boats joined *U178* at Penang, replenishing at sea from tankers during their

operations, and sank 17 ships from January–May 1944. Reinforcement of the submarine forces in the Indian Ocean was now by single boats, transferred from the Atlantic, rather than by whole groups; the incoming craft were mostly Type IX-D2s, long-range boats with an endurance of 42,619km (23,700nm). The homeward and outward-bound U-boats were frequently attacked by British submarines in the Straits of Malacca, without much success, but on 23 September 1944 HMS *Trenchant* sank the *U859* inbound for Penang.

Many of the U-boats returning from the Indian Ocean now carried cargoes of vital raw materials, but few reached their destination, which was generally Norway. On 6 October 1944, for example, *U168* was sunk north of Java by the Dutch submarine *Zvaardfish*; *U537* was sunk north of Bali by the US submarine *Flounder* on 9 November; and *U196* vanished in the Sunda Strait, never to be seen again.

ABOVE *U-boats in the process of construction, seen at the Hamburg shipyards of Blohm und Voss after the town's capture by troops of the British Second Army. Despite the devastation caused to Hamburg by air raids, the shipyards were still functioning at the war's end.*

The last U-boats to operate in the Indian Ocean began returning to their home bases on 6 January 1945, when the *U510* (Lieutenant-Commander Eick) sailed from Jakarta. On 24 April she was forced to put into St Nazaire, short of fuel. On 13 January, *U532* (Commander Junker) also sailed, sinking a tanker and a freighter in the Atlantic in March; on 10 May she entered Liverpool flying the flag of surrender.

The *U843* (Lieutenant-Commander Herwatz) and *U861* (Commander Oesten) both reached Bergen in April; but the last boat to set out, the *U183*, was sunk in the Java Sea by the US submarine Besugo on 24 April, a fortnight before Germany's capitulation.

INDEX